Top SKI RESORTS *of* THE WORLD

Top SKI RESORTS *of* THE WORLD

BARRON'S

ARNIE WILSON

First edition for the United States
and Canada published by
Barron's Educational Series, Inc., 2002.

First published in 2002 by New Holland
Publishers, London, U.K.

All inquiries should be addressed to:
Barron's Educational Series, Inc.
250 Wireless Boulevard
Hauppauge, New York 11788
http://www.barronseduc.com

International Standard Book No:
0-7641-5545-8
Library of Congress Catalog Card No:
2001098843

Publishers' Acknowledgments
New Holland Publishers would like to
thank the Ski Club of Great Britain, and
in particular Vanessa Haines, for their
assistance with this title.

Publisher Mariëlle Renssen
Commissioning Editor Claudia dos Santos
Managing Editors Claudia dos Santos
and Mari Roberts
Managing Art Editor Richard MacArthur
Designer Geraldine Cupido
Editor Ingrid Schneider
Cartographers Elaine Fick, Genené Hart
and Elmari Kuyler
Picture Researcher Karla Kik
Proofreader/Indexer Sean Fraser
Consultant Ski Club of Great Britain
Production Myrna Collins

Reproduction by
Hirt & Carter (Pty) Ltd, Cape Town

Printed in Singapore
9 8 7 6 5 4 3 2 1

Author's Dedication
For Vivianne, my wife

HALF TITLE A lone skier lets rip at Lagazuoi, one of the most beautiful locations in Cortina's portfolio of ski areas.

FULL TITLE Deep, crisp, and even – early snow in Val d'Isère, just in time for the opening of the World Cup races.

RIGHT Far from the madding crowd: a helicopter takes skiers to untracked powder fields.

OVERLEAF Taking off-piste to extremes – "big air" is the ultimate challenge.

N186EH

Contents

FOREWORD

AS A DOWNHILL RACER, skiing has been my life – but there is much more to it than just winning races. After I won the Olympic Downhill at Innsbruck in 1976, people would sometimes feel uneasy about skiing with me in case they could not keep up – until I reassured them that skiing is all about having fun and doesn't have to be done at breakneck speed. I like to stop and admire the view, too!

I have known Arnie for many years, but we didn't ski together until 1991 when I ran a race-training camp at Copper Mountain. He was a devoted pupil and I think I managed to iron out one or two of his faults. So far, he hasn't produced any Olympic medals, but if you could win one for enthusiasm, he would be a strong contender.

Since then we have skied together many times, and share the view – in common with most skiers – that just being in the mountains with a few friends, taking in the fresh air and the beautiful scenery, making turns together, and enjoying a schnapps or a gluhwein afterward, is what the sport – and this book – is really all about. There are one or two places in *Top Ski Resorts of the World* that I haven't skied yet, but having read about them, I am inspired to visit. Like Arnie, my legs and my soul are always hungry for more. I hope this book will inspire you, too, to explore the best ski resorts in this wonderful world of ours.

FRANZ KLAMMER
OLYMPIC CHAMPION
Vienna 2002

RIGHT The "Kaiser's" Hahnenkamm, Kitzbühel, Austria. Franz Klammer won the world's most feared downhill four times – a record no other skier has ever equaled.

BLIZZARD
BLIZZARD
BLIZZARD-FANS
Klammer, Resch & Co
14

KINDERHUT
KINDERHUT
33

INTRODUCTION

THOSE WHO SKI OR SNOWBOARD REGULARLY WILL NEED NO convincing as to what an extraordinary and exhilarating experience it can be. Those who have never tried it may wonder what all the fuss is about. The "fuss" cannot be overstated. There are very few outdoor pursuits that, with the help of that all-important component, gravity – and snow, of course – reward participants with such extreme pleasure. And few that you would want to pursue from dawn till dusk. Whether you emerge from a cozy chalet after a hearty breakfast to find yourself cruising down pistes groomed to "corduroy" perfection, or floating through deep powder like a weightless astronaut, you can hardly fail to be elated. Sometimes it can come very close to being a spiritual event. Buzz Aldrin, one of the first men on the moon, learned to ski long after his moon walk and wishes he had started younger.

But first you have to learn. Any budding Hermann Maier or Jonny Moseley needs to spend as many hours on the snow as possible before skiing or riding becomes intuitive and effortless. Just as a would-be astronaut cannot embark on a space walk without being thoroughly trained at NASA, anyone who wants to ski or snowboard must learn the basics – fortunately nowhere near as daunting as preparing for a space mission.

You can ski on all five continents. So there are, of course, many breathtaking mountain ranges where you can practice this enthralling sport – year-round if you want to. By traveling between the two hemispheres you can enjoy as many back-to-back winters as you care for.

There is, in my opinion, no such thing as a bad ski resort. As Friedl Pfeifer, the great Austrian ski pioneer, once told me when I tried to draw him out on which of the ski runs he had cut at Aspen, Colorado, were his favorites, "They all got something for someone."

As yet, not all the world's mountain ranges have major ski resorts – particularly in the obscure regions of central Asia. But there is first-rate skiing in the Alps, the Pyrenees, the Rockies, the Appalachians, the Andes, the Japan Alps, New Zealand's Southern Alps, and Australia's Snowy Mountains.

While ski resorts in India and Georgia (in the former USSR) tend to be small, patchy, or antiquated, there is magnificent helicopter skiing in Himachal Pradesh, as well as in Kashmir (if the political climate is stable) and the Caucasus. Well off the beaten track, there is also excellent skiing to be had in Iran, Lebanon, and Korea. Even China has a rapidly growing ski industry. In the Andes, where organized skiing is pretty much confined to Chile and Argentina, there is an astonishingly high ski lift at Chacaltaya, soaring over 5500m (18,000ft) above the Bolivian capital, La Paz. There is skiing in Morocco's Atlas Mountains, and – to many people's surprise – the Drakensberg range in South Africa, which reaches 3482m (11,425ft), is home to one of the oldest ski clubs in the world, even though they do not always get sufficient snow to ski!

The ski areas we feature in this book focus on this astonishing global diversity. Some, such as Manali in the Himalaya, Valdez in Alaska, and Blue River in the wilderness of British Columbia, are not really "resorts" at all, but mountain communities from which helicopters take skiers and snowboarders soaring to virginal peaks. Here, far from the madding crowd, they can spend hours, days, or even weeks, skiing in pristine, untracked snow. Some resorts, such as Verbier in Switzerland, Val d'Isère in France, and Kitzbühel in Austria, are old favorites that feature in many major tour operators' brochures. Others, such as Las Leñas in Argentina and Valdez, Alaska, are less likely to be on the average family's skiing list. We hope that our presentation of these superb ski locations will appeal to "real" skiers and armchair skiers alike. Somewhere in the world right now, virgin snowfields await fresh tracks. It could be your turn. And one good turn, as we all know, deserves another.

Arnie Wilson

ARNIE WILSON

Haywards Heath, West Sussex, England, 2002

TOP LEFT Sometimes skiing is all about pausing to admire the view in special, almost spiritual places. The Tasman Glacier at Aoraki/Mount Cook, New Zealand, provides a moment to treasure.

FAR LEFT Skiers hurtle down The Bear – it's skiing, but not as most of us know it. If you tackle Valdez at its steepest, prepare to be very afraid!

TOP RIGHT A simple tool for a whole lot of fun – these skis will go anywhere from bunny slopes to cliff leap. Choose any pair – the rest is entirely up to you.

CENTER: They take skiing seriously in Colorado, even at this tender age. The Kinderhut ski school at Breckenridge hopes one of these youngsters could be a future Olympian.

BOTTOM RIGHT: Gone skiin'! It may look like a day to stay at home, but it takes more than a storm to keep eager skiers off the mountain. Sometimes the best days happen in falling snow.

EUROPE

VAL D'ISERE & TIGNES, COURCHEVEL & THE TROIS VALLEES, CHAMONIX & ARGENTIERE,
LES ARCS & LA PLAGNE, LA GRAVE & LES DEUX ALPES
ST. ANTON-AM-ARLBERG, KITZBÜHEL, ISCHGL
ZERMATT, VERBIER, ST. MORITZ, DAVOS & KLOSTERS, ANDERMATT
GARMISCH-PARTENKIRCHEN
CORTINA D'AMPEZZO, SELVA & VAL GARDENA
ÅRE, RIKSGRÄNSEN

Europe is the cradle of skiing. The Alps are the mountains that most skiers and snowboarders know best, and often love most. Unlike many ski areas elsewhere, the great classic resorts here, like Val d'Isère in France and Austria's St. Anton, are household names to most winter vacationers. Who has not heard of St. Moritz, perhaps the best-known winter sports resort in the world? Or marveled at Mont Blanc, the fearsome giant of Chamonix, and Zermatt, with its mighty Matterhorn?

The majestic peaks of the Alps are where skiing's colossi – Sailer and Schranz, Killy and Klammer, and then Maier – earned their spurs. Before the days of jet travel opened up more distant and exotic mountain horizons, the Alps were unquestionably the Holy Grail of the skiing world. For many aficionados they remain so to this day.

LEFT A rustic oasis in the Trois Vallées' vast purpose-built *domaine de ski*. Even Saulire, at the heart of the region's state-of-the-art modern lift system complex, has its beauty spots.

VAL D'ISERE & TIGNES

SAVOIE, FRANCE

THE BEST BIRTHDAY PRESENT I EVER HAD WAS FROM a young Alsace schoolteacher called Daniel spending his vacation as a ski instructor in Val d'Isère. His present? Opening my eyes to the true glory of the off-piste possibilities of "Val" and its neighbor, Tignes (jointly known as L'Espace Killy in honor of France's greatest skier, Jean-Claude Killy). In one unparalleled week almost 20 years ago, Daniel took us on a tour of some of the greatest "ski-sauvage" arenas in the Alps. The snow was near perfect. The only time we touched a piste was to get from one exhilarating off-piste area to another. We discovered couloirs. We discovered, in a way, ourselves.

This is not to say, of course, that you have to face your fears to enjoy L'Espace Killy. You do not even have to go off-piste in the first place, although it is what both these resorts are famous for. Of the two, Val d'Isère, once a small hunting village owned by the Dukes of Savoie, is more traditional, with an old quarter complete with an ancient church dating back to 1553. Since the 1992 Winter Olympics, the village has almost reinvented itself, adding attractive wood and stone buildings.

Tignes, by consensus, has rather less charm. To be fair, it is not the original. Until 1952, the delightful old village of Tignes was to be found just above Les Brévières but it was "drowned" by a huge artificial lake, the Lac de Chevril, installed to provide hydroelectric power.

One of the better ways of orientating yourself in Val d'Isère is to take the Funival funicular to Bellevarde. Famous for its 1992 Olympic downhill, it is also a wide plateau with a network of enjoyable blue and green runs.

TOP All aboard the high-speed Funival funicular – the quick way to the top of Bellevarde, at the heart of Val d'Isère's ski circuit. Its twin in Tignes takes just six minutes to reach the top.

RIGHT L'Espace Killy is an off-piste paradise, although sometimes you have to work a little to reach the powder – manageable if you're on skis, but snowboarders beware.

Skiing to your right, away from the Bellevarde face, you can choose between the Mont Blanc, Verte, "3J," and Diebold pistes for a fairly gentle warm-up run down toward La Daille. If you feel like something more testing, you could try Orange or the 5km (3-mile) OK World Cup run normally used for the annual "Critérium de la Première Neige" – traditionally Europe's opening World Cup races.

Solaise is the gateway both to some gentle slopes off the Madeleine, Datcha, and Glacier lifts, and an entirely different valley, the Vallon de L'Iseran, dominated by long, wide-open intermediate terrain. Apart from its famous bump run, Solaise is also the departure point for some interesting tree skiing, much of it with off-piste variants, down to Le Laisinant.

From Le Fornet, the furthest lift-served point of Val d'Isère's skiing along the valley floor, you can also reach the Pissaillas glacier from which there are some excellent off-piste runs down to the Haute Maurienne and the remote village of Bonneval. There are also gentle off-piste runs toward the Pays Désert and various descents ending up at the Fornet cable car.

Sooner or later, skiers and boarders will want to venture over to Tignes. This can be achieved by either taking the frequently busy Tommeuses lifts or the Borsat Express chair. Once "over the top" you'll find an area just as extensive as Val d'Isère waiting to be explored.

Tignes has its own funicular from Val Claret up to the spectacular Grande Motte glacier where, until recently, the slopes were open 365 days a year. Because of what appears to be global warming, the glacier now shuts down for a period each summer. The top of the Grande Motte ski area, at 3456m (11,340ft) is reached by cable car. It can be very cold, so dress warmly. The runs down the broad snowfield are long and mainly easy, although with a combination of moguls and icy conditions the descent can be slightly daunting. Do not stray off-piste here without knowing what you are doing. This is a glacier, which is perfectly safe if you stick to the marked slopes, but there are crevasses not far away, particularly in lean snow years.

Apart from the 300km (190 miles) of pistes shared between Val d'Isère and Tignes, there are almost endless permutations of off-piste itineraries. DO hire a guide. The Tour de Charvet is a good intermediate off-piste tour to start off with. If you want something more challenging, try the Face de Charvet (guide essential). The gladed chutes above Lavancher are good but can be avalanche-prone. Super L can be beautiful in good snow. Since the opening of the Cugnai chairlift, the Vallon de Cugnai – a long, sweeping, glorious off-piste valley – has become a great favorite. La Spatule, a wonderful off-piste variant from the north face of Bellevarde down to La Daille, is another outstanding descent in good snow. And that is just Val d'Isère. In Tignes, the list goes on. And on.

Meanwhile, what of beginners? Well, there is plenty for them here but, as John Yates-Smith, one of the resort's local cognoscenti said once, "Beginners tend to think of Val d'Isère the way a schoolboy thinks of Liz Hurley – a tad ambitious for a first experience."

ABOVE Val d'Isère hosted the key men's Alpine events in the 1992 Albertville Winter Olympics, including the controversial Bellevard downhill won by Patrick Ortlieb of Austria, whose style was likened at the time to "a cement truck with power steering."

RESORT	VAL D'ISERE & TIGNES
GETTING THERE:	Geneva airport and heliport: 165km (100 miles); Chambéry airport: 130km (80 miles). Train services from Chambéry to Bourg St. Maurice. Bourg St. Maurice to Val d'Isere: 30km (20 miles); heliport at resort.
HEIGHT:	Tignes: 1550–3660m (5090–12,000ft) Val d'Isère: 1850–3660m (6070–12,000ft)
NO. OF LIFTS:	Tignes: 47; Val d'Isère: 50
TYPES OF PISTES:	15% beginner, 47% intermediate, 38% advanced.
MAIN ADVANTAGES:	Long season; huge ski area; excellent off-piste.
DRAWBACKS:	Most skiing above tree line; Tignes purpose-built.

COURCHEVEL & THE TROIS VALLEES

SAVOIE, FRANCE

IN THIS SAHARA OF SNOW, SKIERS AND BOARDERS can undertake the ultimate ski safari. If you want to ski till you drop – this is the place. It is generally accepted that Courchevel and the neighboring resorts in France's celebrated Trois Vallées – Méribel, Les Menuires, Val Thorens, the Maurienne Valley, Saint-Martin-de-Belleville, and La Tania – comprise the largest ski "domaine" in the world. Depending on where you stay, it can also be one of the most expensive.

With its assorted boutiques, jewelers and nightclubs, Courchevel is in some ways a microcosm of the French capital and has been described as "Paris on Ice" or the "21st arrondissement." The undisputed capital of this vast snowy kingdom even has its own little airport, right on the slopes. Hiring a helicopter from Geneva or Lyon will leave you little change from £1000, but the 30-minute flight by plane from Geneva is more affordable at around £80 ($120) per passenger.

Unlike so many modern French resorts, Courchevel was built just after the War. Although always regarded as chic, it was not a particularly pretty sight until it enjoyed a facelift in preparation for the 1992 Winter Olympics, when many of the concrete buildings were given sloping roofs and wooden cladding. It is important that Courchevel has a huge skiing area of its own because it is not uncommon for the lifts linking it with Méribel and the rest of the circuit to be closed in bad weather. Even just skiing at Courchevel 1650 (named, as are the other villages, after its height in meters) gives you considerable variety, especially with a guide or instructor to lead you to a few "secret" spots. In the vicinity of Les Avals, Roc Merlet, Le Signal, and a whole clutch of insignificant-looking Poma lifts around Bel

TOP A jewel in the clouds: Courchevel 1850, sometimes known as "Paris on Ice" – the highest and most exclusive of the four villages that make up this chic Olympic resort.

RIGHT Although Courchevel is at the far end of the Trois Vallées, high-speed lifts enable reasonably experienced skiers and snowboarders to reach Val Thorens and beyond, and still return in time for tea.

CHALET
DES 2 LACS

Air, Pyramides, and Chanrossa, there is a truly surprising amount of challenging skiing, including the Canyon and the wonderfully wild, steep-sided ravine lurking near Praméruel, which drops into the Ruisseau d'Ariondaz.

In Courchevel alone, there are endless choices. Even about where to sleep. Do you stay at 1850, the highest, most expensive, and most chic of Courchevel's four villages? Or bustling 1650, literally more down to earth, cheaper, with its own excellent ski area – still linked, of course, with 1850 and the rest of the Trois Vallées? There is also a Courchevel 1300, better known as Le Praz, where a handful of Courchevel's finest gourmet restaurants are located. On those wild, white-out days when the weather finally gets the better of you, nothing is more satisfying than skiing down to Le Praz for a very long lunch. In such conditions the tree-lined runs are a delight. Although skiing in continuously falling snow provides its own special magic, it also encourages skiers to linger longer in mountain restaurants.

The skiing permutations in the Trois Vallées are seemingly unlimited. The statistics are difficult to take in, and certainly impossible to ski in a week. At the last count there were 600km (380 miles) of skiing, 207 lifts, 1400 snow cannons, 46 easy runs, 170 medium runs, and 35 difficult runs – including Courchevel's three celebrated couloirs, the Grand, Sous Téléphérique, and Emile Allais. Because these chutes are, rather unusually, marked on the piste map, it would be a serious mistake to assume that they are not challenging, and sometimes dangerous. Although Courchevel and neighboring Méribel are famous for miles of beautifully groomed cruising pistes, they are also renowned for their off-piste runs, too numerous to describe in detail. One classic is the beautiful Les Avals valley, reached by hiking up from the top of the Chanrossa chair lift.

In spite of the vast choice of off-piste opportunities in the Trois Vallées, it is a safe bet that it is those 170 medium runs that make the area so incredibly popular with the vast majority of skiers: the intermediates.

Assuming the weather is favorable and you want to move around the Trois Vallées, let us consider the various possibilities. Your first port of call could be Méribel, a pretty but faintly cutesy collection of villages founded by an Englishman Peter Lindsay. Méribel, which markets itself as "Méribel, very belle!" and "The Heart of the Alps," has its own extensive ski area, including some excellent off-piste itineraries, and France's first eight-seat chair lift.

From Méribel you could make a worthwhile detour to the delightful old-world village of Saint-Martin-de-Belleville, before continuing to its antithesis, the unfortunately named Les Menuires. It is indeed a rather ugly place, although as a defensive French friend once put it: "You can get used to anything." Again, Les Menuires has ample skiing of its own, including La Masse, across the Vallée de Belleville, a huge face with quite tough skiing and a number of off-piste opportunities, including the excellent Itinéraire du Lou. Les Menuires, in turn, is linked with moody and magnificent Val Thorens, at 2300m (7550ft) the highest ski resort in the Alps. This rather bleak place has mainly strong-intermediate to hard-core skiing (and some easier slopes) but is not one I would recommend for novices. The off-piste is challenging and varied, and with a high-mountain guide, there are all kinds of ski-touring opportunities. One of these is the Glacier Gebroulaz. Tiring to reach, but not too difficult to ski, it takes you into Méribel through the back door. One thing is certain – whatever standard of skier or snowboarder you are, it is extremely unlikely that you will exhaust the possibilities in the Trois Vallées. Even if you spend the rest of your life there.

LEFT Val Thorens: not the prettiest of the Trois Vallées resorts, but the highest and usually the most snow-sure, with some of the most challenging runs and best off-piste opportunities.

TOP RIGHT All set for a good winter season in Courchevel, gateway to the legendary Trois Vallées – the most chic but not the cheapest resort in the French Alps.

RESORT	COURCHEVEL & THE TROIS VALLEES
GETTING THERE:	Geneva airport: 145km (90 miles); Chambéry airport: 115km (70 miles); Moûtiers: 25km (15 miles). Bus, train, taxi services from Chambéry. Air, bus, and taxi services from Geneva to Courchevel.
HEIGHT:	Courchevel: 1300–2740m (4270–8990ft) Trois Vallées: 1300–3200m (4270–10,500ft)
NO. OF LIFTS:	Courchevel: 67; Trois Vallées: 190
TYPES OF PISTES:	291 pistes covering 600km (370 miles). Trois Vallées: 27% beg, 61% inter, 12% adv.
MAIN ADVANTAGES:	Huge ski area of Courchevel, Méribel, and Val Thorens; fast modern lift system; variety of village styles.
DRAWBACKS:	Some villages are unattractive; can be busy at peak times; few tree-level runs.

CHAMONIX & ARGENTIERE

HAUTE SAVOIE, FRANCE

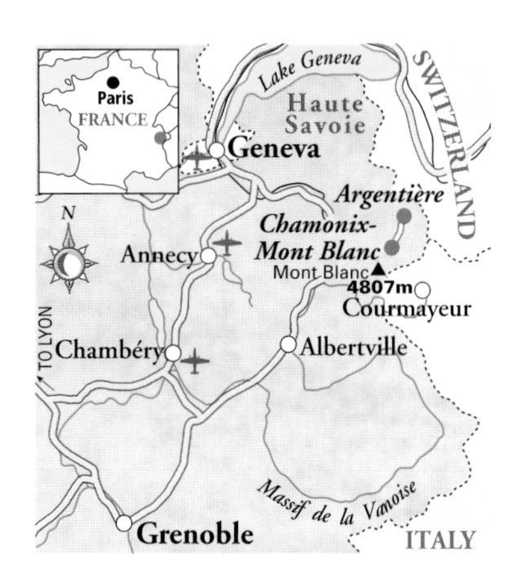

BOTH CROWNED AND DWARFED BY MONT BLANC (4807m; 15,772ft), the highest mountain in the Alps, Chamonix is regarded by many as the "cradle" of climbing. With its generous collection of glaciers tumbling into the Mer de Glace, it also offers some of the most dramatic and, for the true extreme skier, scarcely believable challenges in the world.

Among the first explorers in the region were two Britons, Richard Pococke and William Windham, who arrived in 1741 fully armed not with ice axes but weapons, expecting to be confronted by "savages." It was almost another half-century, in 1786, before two locals, Dr. Michel-Gabriel Paccard and Jacques Balmat, reached the top of the mountain long assumed to be both evil and unconquerable.

Even today, a strange and heady mixture of excitement, foreboding, and even a little mysticism greets skiers and riders as they approach this picturesque climbing center, craning their necks for a view of the sublime Mont Blanc massif, high above the Arve Valley. From Chamonix, Mont Blanc itself is barely visible behind a ring of jagged peaks that, like sentinels of granite, appear to guard it from the town: Dôme du Goûter, Mont Maudit, and Mont Blanc du Tacul, all well over 4000m (13,000ft), dominate the skyline. Even the celebrated Aiguille du Midi, the start of one of the greatest off-piste adventures in Europe – the Vallée Blanche – rears up dramatically to 3842m (12,605ft).

The slopes in the Chamonix Valley are scattered among half a dozen areas, few of which actually link. There is a bus service, but a car is preferable. Other resorts within range include Megève, Les Houches, and St. Gervais. Courmayeur, in a spectacular setting on the Italian side of Mont

TOP The train station at Chamonix. Skiing aficionados arrive by rail, air, and road. Geneva is only 80km (50 miles) away and there is a direct TGV (speed train) link from Paris on weekends.

RIGHT Snow falls generously in the Chamonix Valley, covering trees and chalets under a luxuriously thick white blanket, ensuring excellent ski conditions and cozy après-ski.

Blanc, is a must, providing the Mont Blanc tunnel is open. Apart from its own ski area and some dramatic descents from the Italian side of the Mont Blanc massif (including an Italian version of the Vallée Blanche), Courmayeur has some excellent helicopter skiing.

In Chamonix, Brévent and Flégère are the two areas most intermediates will head for. Between them they have plenty of relaxed, enjoyable skiing, with some more challenging runs thrown in. The cable car ride from Planpraz to the top of Brévent (2525m; 8285ft) is spectacular unless you do not have a head for heights. There is no easy way down; unless you take the cable car down again, you have a choice between a black and a red run. The Le Tour end of the valley, with lifts up to the Col de Balme, offers quite extensive skiing and boarding, mainly above the tree line, with a great deal of wide-open off-piste opportunities. You can even ski across the Swiss border down to Vallorcine and catch the train back.

Many strong skiers and boarders head straight for Argentière's vast Grands Montets, which offer some of the finest skiing and boarding in Europe, for the duration of their stay. Apart from Les Chosalets, a small area 500m (1600ft) from the main Grands Montets lift system with easy, wide-open slopes for beginners, Argentière is predominantly high-intermediate to expert terrain. A two-stage cable car takes skiers and boarders to the "sharp end" of the mountain (3275m; 10,745ft). By getting out at Lognan, the halfway stage, or taking the chair lift to Grand Joran, you can access a number of good lift and piste options, including a ride to the top of the Bochard Gondola with its thrilling Chamois descent.

From the top station, there is a wonderful view of the Aiguille du Dru and the Aiguille Verte (4121m; 13,521ft). Couloirs on these seemingly impossible peaks have, unbelievably, been skied by Yves Detry and the late Jean-Marc Boivin, extreme skiers with whom I have been fortunate enough to spend a number of days in the Alps.

Apart from two serious off-piste routes, which should be attempted only with a guide, there are only two ways to start the long descent (2035m; 6677ft) from the top of the Grands Montets: the tough, black ungroomed runs of Point de Vue and Pylones. On the lower stages of Point de Vue you can enjoy a ringside view of the awe-inspiring Glacier d'Argentière. Some guides will even take you a little way onto the glacier to enable you to make one or two careful turns among the séracs. Trying this, or the thrilling Pas de Chèvre (Goat's Hop), without a guide is foolhardy.

TOP LEFT Don't look down! Even hardened skiers can suffer from vertigo while crossing the bridge from the top of the cable car to the start of the Vallée Blanche.

LEFT The awe-inspiring Aiguille du Midi. Skiers resemble a trail of ants on this unnerving ridge, which puts many people off doing one of the world's longest off-piste descents.

The highlight of your travels in Chamonix is likely to be the cable car ride to the impossibly steep and spiny Aiguille du Midi. This journey is mind-boggling even without skis, as thousands of tourists discover each year. Building a cable car to such a craggy eyrie was a hugely demanding and dangerous operation; the steel cable, more than a mile long, had to be carried up by 20 mountain guides. Two of them died in the process.

The exit to the cable car is linked by a short causeway to the beginning of the legendary Vallée Blanche. Anyone suffering from vertigo should return immediately – the downward views are almost overwhelming. There are three or four principal routes down the Vallée Blanche, all of which involve a rather hair-raising trudge down a ridge to a flattish plateau, carrying your skis and usually roped together.

The main "tourist" route, contrary to rumor, is easy, and the only reason – albeit a good one – for a guide is to avoid the very real threat of crevasses. The scenery on the way down – myriad granite spires, steeples, and towering, jagged peaks – is truly astonishing.

Skiers and boarders can also choose from more adventurous routes, including the so-called *"vraie"* Vallée Blanche, and the Envers du Plan. In good snow these are excellent powder descents, occasionally calling for roped descents of small ice walls. Whichever route you take, the first descent of the Vallée Blanche is guaranteed to be more than memorable. Just like Chamonix itself.

RESORT	CHAMONIX & ARGENTIERE
GETTING THERE:	Lyon: 220km (135 miles); Geneva 80km (50 miles); airport bus available; train station in resort, on the St. Gervais–Le Fayet/Vallorcine line. Direct TGV (fast train) link from Paris at weekends.
HEIGHT:	1040–3840m (3410–12,600ft)
NO. OF LIFTS:	49
TYPES OF PISTES:	23% beg, 63% inter, 14% adv.
MAIN ADVANTAGES:	Large, varied ski areas; excellent off-piste; lively après-ski; traditional town; beautiful scenery.
DRAWBACKS:	Ski areas widely spread out; very little slope-side accommodations. Popularity can mean long lines.

RIGHT With glaciers always on the move, the dramatic scenery in the Vallée Blanche is constantly changing and can provide unexpected obstacles and hazards. Sometimes skiers have to be roped down small ice walls. Larger walls sometimes provide them with a novel view of the route ahead, like here, through a snow window.

LES ARCS & LA PLAGNE

SAVOIE, FRANCE

A LITTLE MORE THAN 40 YEARS AGO, SOON AFTER the Americans had elected John F. Kennedy president, the East Germans had erected the Berlin Wall, and the Russians had sent the first man, Yuri Gagarin, into space, the French made a big mistake. Very big. They started building one of the ugliest ski resorts in the world: La Plagne.

One of the first buildings was Aime La Plagne, a monstrous edifice rising like some Alpine Battlestar Galactica from a snowy sea. Plagne Centre was another early construction. Unappealing in architecture, they are surrounded by a wonderful panorama of mountain peaks that somehow lessen the impact. And there are phenomenal amounts of skiing. La Plagne, like a space city with its own suburban satellites and at least 2.5 million "skier days," has arguably become the single most-visited ski area in the world – even more so with its planned new link to neighboring Les Arcs.

The earliest of the so-called "third generation" French ski resorts, La Plagne probably encouraged other resorts, like Flaine, and, some would say, Avoriaz and Les Arcs, to go for brave new world, space-age architecture with little concern for tradition or charm.

Fortunately, the designers at La Plagne had second thoughts about their approach, and as the years went by there were serious attempts at damage control. As more satellite villages were added, the initial harsh architecture tended to be replaced with neorustic. Although Plagne Bellecôte was more of the same, Belle Plagne, Plagne 1800, Plagne Villages, and Plagne Soleil have gone a long way to soften the blow inflicted by earlier planners.

TOP There is so much to see and so many villages to ski in these two resorts that if you venture into the vast off-piste areas you could be anywhere. This skier is approaching Montchavin-Les Coches in perfect powder.

LEFT The monstrous structure of Aime La Plagne is an eyesore from every angle, but La Plagne aficionados say you can get used to anything. And, in a way, they would miss it if it wasn't there.

La Plagne has every conceivable permutation of piste and off-piste, from exhilarating descents on the huge, sweeping glacier at Bellecôte (3000m; 10,000ft), to delightful cruising down quiet, meandering, larch-lined avenues to the charming villages of Montchavin-Les Coches, Champagny-en-Vanoise, and Montalbert. In between these two extremes is La Plagne's biggest attraction for intermediate skiers anxious to cruise till they drop: seemingly endless, wide-open motorway skiing.

Having extended its empire to 10 different villages, La Plagne is planning to send a tentacle across the valley between Montchavin and Peisy Vallandry (an outpost of La Plagne's equally illustrious neighbor, Les Arcs) to form what will be arguably the third biggest ski "domaine" on the planet.

In a world that sees very few new ski resorts, it is particularly exciting when two existing ski areas forge a link – particularly such major resorts as Les Arcs and La Plagne. The prospect of being able to ski from one to the other is certainly stimulating. However, since La Plagne in particular is already so extensive, it is difficult to imagine skiers and boarders of less than average ability being able to exploit the new link.

Les Arcs – whose connection by funicular with the Eurostar train terminal at Bourg St. Maurice makes it the most accessible high-altitude French resort – has always been at the cutting edge of skiing and snowboarding. It pioneered "ski evolutif," a technique for fast learning by progressing quickly from very short skis to longer ones. It became the principal home of the Kilomètre Lancée in which daredevils on huge 237cm (8ft) skis, clad in thin aerodynamic plastic suits and "Darth Vader"-style visors, speed down a special track at breakneck speeds approaching 240kph (150mph). Later the course opened to motorbikes and mountain bikes, too.

ABOVE *Doucement* does it: a "softly softly" approach from the planners of Belle Plagne helped create a more attractive profile for the new-world ski factory resort of La Plagne.

Like La Plagne, Les Arcs has acres of good cruising, but its off-piste opportunities are exceptional. The Aiguille Rouge, which dominates the resort, has some challenging runs down its front face (best skied with a guide) and is also the starting point for one of the longest descents in the Alps. The largely black run down to the charming little village of Villaroger is well over 16km (10 miles) long.

Those in search of a real away-from-it-all treat will enjoy climbing up and over the Grand Col, pausing at the top to admire the superb panorama of French, Swiss, and Italian peaks, including Mont Blanc, Monte Rosa, and a glimpse of the Matterhorn. A magnificent plunge down the glacier leads into a wonderful collection of snowfields on the Réserve Naturelle des Hauts de Villaroger. The route continues down to the village of Le Planay, an exhilarating vertical drop of almost 2000m (6500ft), and then back to Les Arcs.

The huge téléphérique that will form the 2km (1¼-mile) link between the satellite villages of Montchavin and Peisy Vallandry will take up to 200 people. There are three separate villages: Arc Pierre Blanche (1600), Arc Chantel (1800), and the bowl area of Arc 2000. When Les Arcs was being built, the planners experienced considerable difficulties associated with Arc 1600 when they discovered the buildings were beginning to slip silently down the mountain as a result of the ground being waterlogged. They were quickly shored up with concrete, but the joke at the time was that Arc 2000 might slip down the mountain too, and become Arc 1800, which itself would slide down to replace Arc 1600. I am happy to report that it never happened. A fourth village, a unique combination of French and Canadian expertise, is due to be built alongside Arc 2000 by Intrawest, the ubiquitous ski resort developer in North America that won considerable praise for reinventing the Quebec resort of Tremblant.

RESORT	LES ARCS & LA PLAGNE
GETTING THERE:	Geneva and Chambéry airport both 150km (95 miles); La Plagne to Aime: 17km (10 miles); Les Arcs to Bourg St. Maurice: 15km (9 miles). Bus, coach, and taxi services from Chambéry airport; train/bus from Aime and Bourg.
HEIGHT:	La Plagne: 1250–3250m (4100–10,660ft) Les Arcs: 1600–2450m (5250–8040ft)
NO. OF LIFTS:	La Plagne: 109; Les Arcs: 76
TYPES OF PISTES:	La Plagne: 9% beg, 86% inter, 5% adv. Les Arcs: 8% beg, 78% inter, 14% adv.
MAIN ADVANTAGES:	La Plagne: large ski area; snow-sure resort. Les Arcs: fast lift system; large ski area.
DRAWBACKS:	La Plagne: limited après-ski; purpose-built central villages. Les Arcs: purpose-built; few hotel accommodations.

LA GRAVE & LES DEUX ALPES

ISERE, FRANCE

IN 1934, MONSIEUR RUDOLPHE TESSA ANNOUNCED that he would buy any automobile capable of climbing the mule track to his hunting lodge at the Alpe de Mont de Lans in the Southern French Alps. A Peugeot accomplished the journey with a special "mountain axle," but according to the archives, "it was necessary to carry the car on the bends."

The first rope tow at what would become known as Les Deux Alpes, installed just before the outbreak of World War II, fell down 15 minutes later. The postwar years were kinder to this French ski resort, which much later linked up with one of the most dramatic climbing and skiing centers in Europe: La Grave. Despite the cliché, the phrase "mean, moody, and magnificent" applies so aptly to the extraordinary ski area of La Grave that I hope I am forgiven for using it. With the exception of Chamonix, there is surely nowhere in the Alps with such startling, almost overwhelming glacial scenery.

When I first wrote about this awe-inspiring place in an earlier book, a colleague laughed good-naturedly at what I had written: "Huge glaciers and moraine fields stare down at you as you ski, feeling like an Alpine Tom Thumb, down the vast snowfields at the base of those jagged peaks." For some winters to come I was referred to as an Alpine Tom Thumb, but to be honest it was not such a bad analogy. Dominated by the jutting form of La Meije (4000m; 13,000ft) it is a fearsomely beautiful place.

The area's statistics – listed in a recent French resort guide under La Meije/La Grave as "1400m–3550m, ski runs 2, ski lifts 4" – are puzzling indeed. How can a ski area be worth visiting if it only has two runs? It is the huge vertical descent of 2150m (7050ft) that gives the game away.

TOP To ski or not to ski? There is always danger from avalanches or crevasses on the fabulous unpisted slopes of La Grave beneath the mighty Meije. The area should not be attempted without a guide, however, and certainly never alone.

RIGHT The picturesque old village of La Grave straggles along the wonderfully scenic Col du Lautaret – a climber's paradise "borrowed" by skiers and snowboarders.

THE NORTH FACE

La Grave is a vast, steep mountainside with no groomed pistes at all. Apart from a tame section at the very top on the Glacier de la Girose, with two T-bars where it "links," so to speak, with the big local destination resort of Les Deux Alpes, the slopes provide an all-consuming, relentless descent from top to bottom. The "ski runs 2" referred to in the French publication – along with their variants – are simply the easiest and safest way down. If you stick to these two runs there is nothing really beyond a strong intermediate skier, but the moment you wander off in any other direction you may have to deal with much steeper terrain, a variety of couloirs and a selection of cliffs, small and large.

In addition to this, on the upper sections, once you have left the easy liaison with Les Deux Alpes, there is potential danger from crevasses and avalanches – all of which adds up to the necessity of hiring a guide. The most hair-raising run I have attempted was the Pan de Rideau (Curtain's Edge). It was not the descent itself that was the most frightening, but the long, quite frankly terrifying traverse to reach it. Unless you are roped to your guide, one slip here and you are gone forever, falling into a vast bowl of sheer and ever-steepening cliffs from which there can be no escape.

From the Dôme de la Lauze, over 3500m (11,400ft) up at the very top of the linked areas, it is also possible (with a guide) to ski a wonderfully scenic and dramatic run down the Vallée de la Selle to the little village of St. Christophe en Oisans.

Originally two separate farming communities – Mont de Lans and Alpe de Venosc – Les Deux Alpes is a mainstream destination resort that provides broad, sweeping slopes, almost entirely above the tree line for all grades of skiers and snowboarders. Plus a vertical drop even more daunting than La Grave's: 2270m (7440ft) if you ski all the way down to the lowest lift at Mont de Lans. Unlike so many ski areas, however, the slopes tend to become easier as they get higher. Thus the lower slopes, immediately above the village nursery slopes, are dominated by steep red runs, with only one – the Chemin des Demoiselles – providing an easy option for novices attempting to return to the village at the end of the day.

The bulk of the rest of this large ski area is dominated by a network of enjoyable blue cruising runs, while high on the Glacier du Mont de Lans the skiing is as much green as blue. This means that after a few days many beginners are able to enjoy wonderful views of Mont Blanc and then ski all the way down from the glacier. There are very few resorts in the world where novices can ski a 14km (9-mile) run during their first week! At the same time, there is plenty of challenging off-piste terrain if you know where to look, or, preferably, take a guide.

The Jandri Express gondola, which can handle almost 2000 passengers an hour, provides the main artery to get the majority of skiers up the mountain to the glacier in some 20 minutes. From here, the Dôme Express funicular takes skiers to the Dôme de la Lauze. The town, or large village, of Les Deux Alpes – a ragtag collection of buildings with a Wild West feel – is not particularly attractive, but by no means as ugly as some French ski resorts. Do make the effort to take a gondola down to picturesque Venosc where you can explore a delightful collection of narrow, cobbled streets, a handful of cozy restaurants, and a scattering of arts and crafts shops – a considerable contrast to the long, sprawling ribbon of development above.

RESORT	LA GRAVE & LES DEUX ALPES
GETTING THERE:	Lyon to Les Deux Alpes: 160km (100 miles); Grenoble to La Grave: 77km (50 miles); Grenoble to Les Deux Alpes: 75km (45 miles). Bus service from Grenoble to Les Deux Alpes.
HEIGHT:	Les Deux Alpes: 1650–3600m (5410–11,810ft) La Grave: 1400–3550m (4600–11,650ft)
NO OF LIFTS:	Les Deux Alpes: 55; La Grave: 4
TYPES OF PISTES:	Les Deux Alpes: 27% beg, 43% inter, 30% adv. La Grave: 15% beg, 85% adv.
MAIN ADVANTAGES:	Les Deux Alpes: High-altitude skiing; modern lift system. La Grave: Quiet resort; huge off-piste area.
DRAWBACKS:	Les Deux Alpes: Most skiing above tree line. La Grave: Small; limited for beginners and intermediates.

ABOVE The two-stage, five-cabin téléphérique on a skyward journey to the Glacier du Vallon from the picturesque village of La Grave.

LEFT Scary slopes. There is no room for error when you ski La Grave; sometimes your guide will rope you up on difficult sections.

ST. ANTON-AM-ARLBERG

TYROL, AUSTRIA

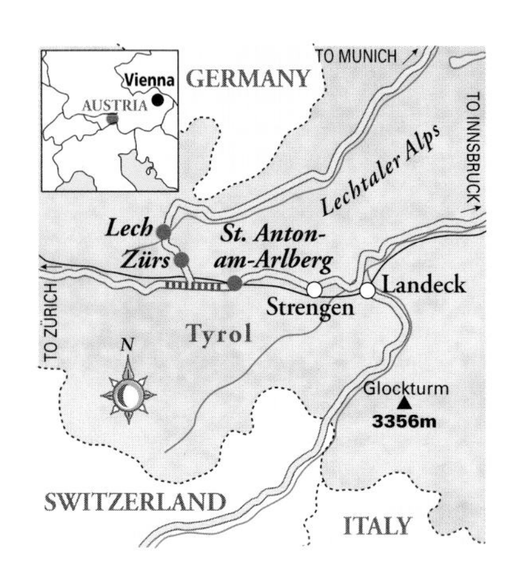

FOR MANY, ST. ANTON-AM-ARLBERG IS BOTH THE cradle and Holy Grail of the skiing and snowboarding world. Ringed by majestic peaks, it has slopes of the highest caliber and a charming old railroad town in which to celebrate the conquest of those slopes. It is also close to other illustrious ski areas – not just Lech and Oberlech, but Zürs, Stuben, and St. Christoph, which are all available on the same lift ticket, giving the region a true embarrassment of riches.

The "white circuit" between Lech, one of the prettiest villages in Austria, and Zürs, is a wonderful day's outing for any skier or boarder with moderate experience. And there's more – across the valley lies Rendl, a completely separate ski arena, with fairly relaxed skiing and a number of more challenging classic off-piste itineraries. The Malfon Valley is a celebrated off-piste excursion, and above Stuben, a hike up the Maroi Kopfe gives access to another, the Maroital. There are sweeping, groomed cruising runs, long, thigh-burning bump runs, daunting but exhilarating couloirs, and magnificent off-piste opportunities including (for brave hearts only) an exciting and severe descent to Zürs from the very top of St. Anton's highest peak, the Valluga (2811m; 9223ft) – only permitted if accompanied by a qualified guide. The Valluga slopes are the focal point for huge areas of off-piste and the starting point for the exhilarating run down to the picturesque village of Stuben, birthplace of the legendary pioneer of the Arlberg technique, Hannes Schneider. Steep but much less daunting are the short, sharp descents through snowfields that filter into the Steissbachtal gully, the great homeward-bound route taken by so many skiers and boarders at the end of a day's adventures.

TOP Don't try this at home. Don't even try this on your ski vacation in St. Anton unless you are genuinely an extreme skier. There is plenty of easier skiing to be found in the beautiful Arlberg region.

RIGHT A packed lunch – sometimes there are so many diners at St. Anton's Ulmer Hütte (2285m; 7495ft) that they spread right across the piste, forcing skiers and snowboarders to make a brief detour on their way down to Stuben.

Ulmer Hütte
2285 m

The story of skiing in St. Anton really starts in neighboring Lech, where a century or more ago it was quite common for the village to be cut off by deep snow for months at a time. In the winter of 1895, the local priest somehow acquired a very long pair of skis to enable him to visit his parishioners. The villagers' amusement turned to interest, and more skis began to appear. But it was not until 1912 that Hannes Schneider, an early pupil of the first ski school in Zürs, devised a way of replacing the time-honored Telemark technique with the soon-to-be famous Arlberg version. When he started his own Arlberg Ski School in 1921, his trademark style became famous around the world.

It was to St. Anton, in 1928, that Schneider's friend Sir Arnold Lunn introduced the famous Arlberg-Kandahar race – a variation of the Roberts of Kandahar Cup race, which had started in Switzerland in 1911 and which was eventually to lead to modern alpine racing. The Arlberg version became the most famous of many Kandahars, which were later held in Garmisch, Quebec, and even Scotland. From 1930 on, the race alternated between St. Anton and Mürren until 1938, when Lunn wrote tersely in his book *The Story of Skiing*: "Nazis occupy Austria. Race cancelled." Although the Arlberg-Kandahar did not return to St. Anton until 1949, it remained the basis for the fearsome Karl Schranz Men's Downhill in the 2001 World Alpine Championships on the steep slopes at Kapall.

Schranz was the subject of one of the most controversial events in the history of ski racing. The three-time world champion was an Olympic silver medalist and declared the world's finest racer on four occasions. What made him a national hero, however, was not winning any medals, but being disqualified from the 1972 Winter Olympics in Sapporo, Japan. Interviewed on the practice slopes of Mount Eniwa, he said: "This thing of amateur

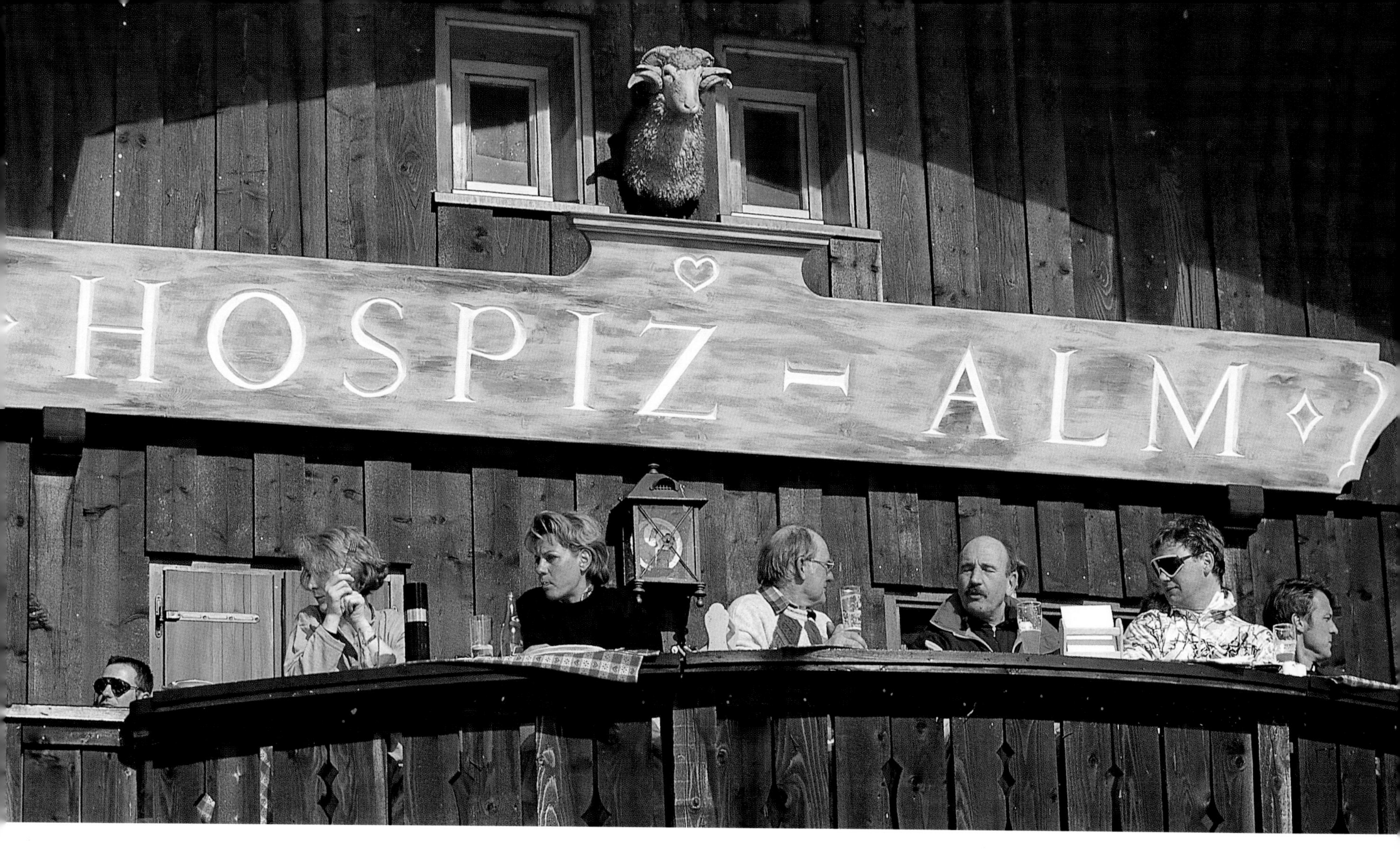

purity is something that dates back to the 19th century when amateur sportsmen were regarded as gentlemen and everybody else was an outcast. The Olympics should be a competition of skill and strength and speed – and no more." For this noble sentiment, which found its way into print in the *Japan Times*, Schranz found himself banned from the Games. He flew home to Vienna to be welcomed by a cheering crowd, estimated at almost a quarter of a million people, who regarded him as a martyr.

Try not to miss a visit – preferably on skis – to the delightful hamlet of St. Christoph, high on the infamous Arlberg Pass. The five-star Hospiz Hotel, built on the site of an ancient hospice where monks rescued travelers overwhelmed by fierce storms, is one of the finest hotels in the Alps and has a 14th-century wine cellar right beneath the church with a collection of some 18,000 bottles. Its more recently constructed companion, the Hospiz-Alm, has the largest known collection of oversized bottles of Bordeaux and Burgundy from famous Chateau estates the world over. "They are worth 62 million Austrian schillings," I was informed by the joint-owner, Adi Werner. "That's almost £3 million. They came into vogue 200 years ago when the Czars were importing wine from Bordeaux to St. Petersburg. They were much easier to ship and less likely to break."

Just think – if you skied to St. Christoph with 80 friends, you could divide one gigantic bottle among you for only a little over £100 a skier!

RESORT	ST. ANTON-AM-ARLBERG
GETTING THERE:	Munich: 220km (135 miles); Zürich: 200km (120 miles); Innsbruck: 95km (60 miles). All major international trains stop at St. Anton's own Eurocity train station. Winter bus services available from Zürich to Lech and Zürs.
HEIGHT:	St. Anton: 1300–2810m (4270–9220ft)
NO. OF LIFTS:	86 in entire network.
TYPES OF PISTES:	260 pisted runs; 200 unpisted routes. 25% beg, 40% inter, 35% adv.
MAIN ADVANTAGES:	Large ski areas; traditional alpine villages; snow-sure slopes.
DRAWBACKS:	Difficult beginner slopes in St. Anton; road to Zürs can close after heavy snow; Lech can be expensive.

OPPOSITE A powder enthusiast on his all-mountain Xscream skis blasts through a cornice on the slopes of the Valluga – this is as good as it gets.

ABOVE The legendary Hospiz-Alm restaurant – famous for its Czar-sized wine bottles – in the bijou village resort of St. Christoph. Don't count on a quick lunch.

PRIMAGAZ
PRIMAGAZ
VOLVO
ratiophar
UNTER DEN BIERE

KITZBÜHEL

TYROL, AUSTRIA

IF YOU SEARCHED THE MOUNTAINS OF THE GLOBE for quintessential Alpine ski-town excitement, you would be hard pressed to improve on the community at Kitzbühel – although at 800m (2600ft) the resort's lack of altitude does sometimes produce anxiety about sufficient snow. There are, however, some 160 snowguns to help things along.

At Kitzbühel, during the week of possibly the most famous and feared downhill competition in the world, the Hahnenkamm, the excitement floods off the Streif run and swirls unstoppably into the pedestrianized center via the narrow cobblestoned streets of this scenic medieval town. Here, to the inevitable strains of some of Austria's strident punk "oompah" bands, the town goes wild – but not in an unseemly way; it is a civilized, benign form of madness. Both on and off the mountain, the highly charged carnival atmosphere is tangible.

Although Kitzbühel has its very own local hero, Toni Sailer (the "Blitz von Kitz" who won three Olympic gold medals at the Cortina d'Ampezzo Games in 1956), another Austrian has made the Hahnenkamm his own. Franz Klammer, the so-called Kaiser of Austrian skiing, is the only person to have won it three years in a row (and four times in all) and is still its undisputed master, even though he has not skied it for almost 20 years. "The Hahnenkamm is the most difficult course by far," he says. "It really sorts out the best skiers from the rest. You need a lot of ability and courage." Bill Johnson, the Olympic downhill champion at Sarajevo in 1984, says, "Anyone who wins here deserves to. There is no way you can cheat a victory."

LEFT Kitzbühel: Holy Grail for downhill racers and balloon enthusiasts alike. An enchanting melange of medieval, baroque, and alpine architecture, Austria's most attractive ski town invokes pleasure and fear in almost equal measure for the world's top skiers.

TOP World-class skiers face their sternest test on the legendary Hahnenkamm – 3.5km (2 miles) of explosive downhill. Franz Klammer – the only man to win it four times – has made the Streif run his own.

RESORT	KITZBÜHEL
GETTING THERE:	Munich: 160km (100 miles); Innsbruck: 100km (60 miles); Salzburg: 80km (50 miles). Airport bus service available from all these airports. Rail and bus services from Salzburg and Munich. Train station at resort.
HEIGHT:	800–2000m (2620–6560ft)
NO. OF LIFTS:	60
TYPES OF PISTES:	39% beg, 42% inter, 19% adv.
MAIN ADVANTAGES:	Beautiful traditional town center; lively après-ski.
DRAWBACKS:	Low altitude leads to unreliable snow; limited advanced skiing; heavy traffic tends to spoil town's charm.

ABOVE Christmas in Kitzbühel, with its medieval walled town center, churches, towers, and town gate, is a magical time, especially after the first winter snows.

It is important to distinguish the Streif run on the Hahnenkamm from the rest of the runs in the Hahnenkamm area, which are nowhere near as fierce. Fortunately for the general public, skiing the Streif run is not obligatory, and certainly not straight down in under two minutes at 130kph (80mph). The start is so steep and icy that racers accelerate to 100kph (60 mph) almost immediately and then take off on the infamous Mausefalle, rushing through the air with a whistling sound like a rifle bullet. To spectators, cheering and clanging huge cowbells, it looks almost vertical.

According to Graham Bell, once one of Britain's top racers and a veteran of five Winter Olympics, even if you survive the terrifying opening moments of the Hahnenkamm, there is only a brief moment when you can relax. "Immediately after the Steilhang, a wall of bulletproof ice, you let out a massive sigh of relief," says Bell. "A nanosecond later, a tight S-bend sets you up for the Hausberg jump. You fly about 20m (60ft) then land close to the fence on the right and turn left into another sharp compression. If you leave it too late, the compression will catapult you off the course."

Vacation skiers and snowboarders can bypass the steepest sections by opting for runs like Asten or Kampen. In fact, you don't even need to go near the Streif – there are plenty of other slopes. If you wish to experience Kitzbühel's "ski safari," take the Hahnenkamm gondola. The safari links "Kitz" with the villages of Pengelstein, Jochberg, Wurzhöhe, Bärenbadkogel, Zweitausender, and, at just over 2000m (6500ft), Resterhöhe and Pass Thurn, where Kitzbühel's best snow and finest skiing can usually be found.

Kitzbühel has two other ski areas, not linked with its main circuit. One of these, the Kitzbüheler Horn, is where skiing in Kitzbühel started. This wonderfully scenic area is noted for long, cruising slopes and has snowboarding inducements like a half-pipe, fun park, and a boardercross course. The other is the tiny but picturesque area of Bichlalm. All these areas are linked by a bus service.

The town of Kitzbühel itself is a real gem. The center is an ancient, medieval walled town with delightful gabled houses, frescos, archways, and color-washed façades. First settled in historic times, it became a major copper-mining center. It was also an important staging post on the shortest route between Bavaria and Venice. The name comes from the Chizzo family, who ruled it in the 12th century, hence "Chizbuhel."

I shall always remember with affection arriving in Kitzbühel from New York's La Guardia Airport one March during an eccentric round-the-world tour that involved skiing every single day of the year. There had been a sigh of relief that it had been possible to ski in Windham, New York, and arrive in Frankfurt in time to ski the following day. In the process, the UK-based coordinator of our expedition, Fran Newitt, had inadvertently invented the first Jewish ski resort in Europe. "They're expecting you," she had faxed, famously, "in Kibutzel."

ISCHGL

TYROL, AUSTRIA

ISCHGL, A BOISTEROUS BUT BEAUTIFUL TYROLEAN village tucked away in the steep-sided Paznaun Valley close to the Swiss border, is one of the best providers of good intermediate cruising in the Austrian Alps. The traffic-free center, dotted with bars, also provides some riotous nightlife. Compared with most other Austrian resorts, Ischgl is a relative newcomer on the scene; it wasn't until 1963 that the first ski lifts were installed.

Centuries ago when Ischgl's Swiss neighbor Samnaun, surrounded by Austria, was essentially cut off from the rest of Switzerland, the villagers struck a deal allowing them huge tax concessions. This inevitably created a smuggler's paradise. The story goes that one villager from the Austrian side of the border, using the traditional excuse of crossing into Switzerland for "a day's hunting," bought a consignment of cigarettes, went straight to Innsbruck without even stopping to sleep, sold the cigarettes for five times what he had paid for them, and, after further tradeoffs, returned to Ischgl with a live ox.

Those very same slopes across which smugglers made their stealthy journeys are now a happy hunting ground for skiers and boarders who like their runs big, wide, and handsome. And with most of Ischgl's slopes above 2000m (6500ft), excellent snow conditions are almost guaranteed.

Ischgl's runs are bewilderingly numerous and some, seemingly endless, coast through stirring scenery. The lifts up to Idalp, the main gateway to the various ski sectors, are busy first thing in the morning, but with three gondolas, the lines move quickly. Once you have arrived at Idalp, a rather

TOP A typical scene in the Alps – and another reason why skiers feel out of this world. The slopes in Ischgl are often way above the clouds that sometimes persist over lowland valleys and towns.

RIGHT Epic skiing in Ischgl – and epic partying afterward. Skiers at this effervescent Austrian party town burn the candle at both ends as they attempt the impossible: to ski every run and visit every bar.

crowded plateau, lifts and runs fan out in most directions. Beginners also start here, which means they have little choice but to descend by gondola again at the end of the day. (Beware: The green run on the trail map, which would signify a nursery slope in the United States, is actually a toboggan run!)

Experts will not find Ischgl overendowed with severe challenges. But everyone else – that great cross section between early intermediate and almost advanced – will be in their element. It almost doesn't matter in which direction you head off.

The high point of the ski area is Palinkopf (2864m; 9396ft). From here there are some wonderfully long, sweeping runs in all directions. One continues all the way down into Samnaun, a popular destination for skiers and boarders who wish to stop for lunch and return with backpacks full of duty-free goods and souvenirs. The return trip involves riding the Pendelbahn, the world's first double-decker cable car, which deposits its passengers at Alp Trida Sattel. From here skiers work their way down the sunny, wide-open slopes to Alp Trida, which links up with the main lift network back to Ischgl via Idjoch. A more direct route from the top of the Pendelbahn straight to Greitspitz was in the pipeline at the time of writing.

From Palinkopf there are also runs down to Fimbatal, above Ischgl, where the Gampenbahn chair makes the return trip back to the Palinkopf again. Other routes take skiers and boarders down a wide gully to Höllenkar from where they can continue back to Idalp.

The Ischgl lift pass covers two other resorts. Galtür, a much quieter village further up the valley, was once favored by Ernest Hemingway. It was devastated by a massive avalanche in 1999, which claimed the lives of 40 people. In the other direction is Kappl, another small but uncrowded resort with superb intermediate slopes and surprisingly good off-piste. It is well worth taking a day to explore the slopes here, particularly at weekends when Ischgl may be crowded.

Ischgl is not the place to go to for a quiet time. The resort is popular with Bavarian skiers who tend to turn the various bars into an unofficial extension of the Munich beer festival. The rustic Kitzloch, where skiers and snowboarders dance on chairs, is almost invariably packed to the hilt. At the Elisabeth Eisbar, you might well witness girls dancing on huge vats of beer outside in the snow. Most skiers start to party without bothering to take their ski boots off, and the roar produced by the various drinking schools would hold its own in a football stadium. One minute they are in good voice at the Pub Treff, only to be drowned out by revelers at the Hotel Ferienglück bar. But all is not lost – there are quieter bars where you can enjoy a nightcap or two far from the madding crowd. The Gasthaus Alt Dorf Café has cows munching away and/or being milked on the floor below. You can watch them through a window, seemingly a picture of contentment. With any luck, you will feel much the same.

RESORT	ISCHGL
GETTING THERE:	Munich: 300km (185 miles); Salzburg: 300km (185 miles); Innsbruck: 100km (60 miles). Bus services available from these airports. Landeck: 30km (20 miles) by rail; frequent bus services from train station.
HEIGHT:	1400–2900m (4600–9510ft)
NO. OF LIFTS:	42
TYPES OF PISTES:	30% beg, 50% inter, 20% adv.
MAIN ADVANTAGES:	Large ski area; snow-sure slopes; lively nightlife.
DRAWBACKS:	Not recommended for beginners; expensive.

OPPOSITE There's plenty more like this; although experts will not find Ischgl overendowed with severe challenges, strong intermediates can cruise all day on a huge network of runs.
ABOVE Skiers pause to study the bewildering selection of runs available at Ischgl before setting off for the day.

ZERMATT

VALAIS, SWITZERLAND

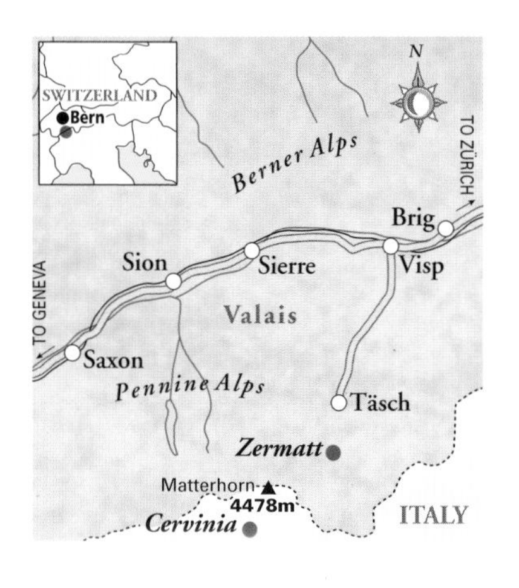

ZERMATT. MATTERHORN. TWO WORDS THAT ARE almost inseparable. No matter where you find yourself on the slopes of this remarkable ski area, the granite monolith of Europe's most famous peak seems to follow you around. Lookalike "Matterhorns" may even follow you around the world; many resorts like to claim a version of this statuesque peak. Mount Assiniboine, for example, in British Columbia, could almost be its twin.

The thrill of the real Matterhorn is complex. At 4478m (14,692ft) it is by no means the highest of the 29 peaks around Zermatt, but its stand-alone, savage beauty commands attention. It is always awe inspiring. On the millions of postcards sent home by skiers from all over the world it can seem idyllic and comfortingly Swiss, but to those climbers who find themselves clinging to its granite walls, it can be a terrible place. Just as the poppy fields of Flanders combine beauty with a fearful past, the Matterhorn, which has taken the lives of so many young climbers, has in some ways the allure of an ancient battlefield. Such thoughts may not preoccupy skiers as they wander the slopes of Zermatt's three distinct areas, but they somehow permeate the ambience of the resort, both in the mountains and in the now rather overgrown village itself.

It was, after all, the first and most tragic ascent of the Matterhorn that made Zermatt – originally "Zer Matt" (The Meadow) – famous around the world. It was on July 14, 1865, that the British climber Edward Whymper, together with a motley collection of fellow-countrymen and

TOP Lit up during winter evenings, the Catholic church in Zermatt offers a striking spectacle as in this view from the balcony of the Hotel Dom.

RIGHT Night falls over Zermatt, nestled beneath the distinctive form of the Matterhorn. The twinkling lights and snow-covered rooftops present a storybook scene to visitors from all over the world.

three mountain guides finally conquered the mountain. It was at least his eighth attempt. Sadly, his triumph was short-lived. Soon after leaving the summit, four of the party plunged to their deaths down the North Face. The body of one, the 18-year-old Lord Francis Douglas, has never been found. The broken hemp rope, plus various grim mementoes of the climb, can be seen in the fascinating local museum.

Almost wherever you find yourself staying in this quaint and bustling village, with its great Seiler Hotels, tearooms, boutiques, and ubiquitous electric buggies (ordinary traffic is banned), you will need to travel a little to reach any one of the three skiing areas. There is an "electrobus" linking the two main gateways – Sunnega and Furi. Perhaps the best and friendliest sector to start with is the "sunny side" of the valley, at Sunnega. This is the gateway to skiing on slopes that reach 3000m (10,000ft) and more: Unterrothorn (3103m; 10,180ft), Stockhorn (3405m; 11,172ft), and most famously, the Gornergrat (3090m; 10,138ft).

Skiers can spy out the land by taking a leisurely but spectacular 45-minute journey by mountain railroad – the first electric rack-and-pinion track in Switzerland – to the Gornergrat. There is a large, quaint hotel at the top, the Kulm, with a wide, sunny terrace overlooking the Gornergletscher and one of the greatest panoramas in the Alps. Almost shoulder to shoulder are the Monte Rosa (4634m; 15,204ft) – in the Alps, second only to Mont Blanc in altitude – Lyskamm, the twin peaks of Castor and Pollux, Breithorn, and the Klein Matterhorn. Here Europe's highest cable car takes skiers and snowboarders to the Italian border, from where they can make their way down to Cervinia in the Aosta Valley.

From the Gornergrat, a clutch of easy blues descends to Riffelberg. The runs from Stockhorn and Unterrothorn down to Blauherd, including Zermatt's celebrated Triftji – tough when moguled, glorious in fresh powder – are more difficult, but from Blauherd back down to Sunnega, the terrain opens out into easy cruising. Other challenging runs in the area include National, Chamois, and Marmotte.

Furi, at the far end of the village, is the gateway to Zermatt's other two areas – the Trockener Steg link to Klein Matterhorn and the Theodulpass, close to the Italian border, and Schwarzsee, near the foot of the Matterhorn. The journey up to Klein Matterhorn is dramatic: the cable car soars above steep glacial terrain to 3885m (12,746ft). At this altitude skiers are urged to take things a little slower. Those traveling down onto the Italian side have the possibility of an exceptionally long run down, not only to Cervinia, but even lower, to the picturesque village of Valtournenche, a distance of at least 20km (12 miles). This obviously means leaving plenty of time for the return journey or facing the expense of a night in the wrong country!

Some of Zermatt's most challenging bump runs are encountered below Schwarzsee, on the way back to Zermatt via Furi. These include Furgg-Furi, Aroleid, and Tiefbach. But intermediates can take the Weisse Perle, a pleasant roller coaster red run as an alternative route. This gives skiers and boarders a wonderful opportunity to visit some of the mountain restaurants for which Zermatt is so deservedly famous. There is a clutch of them around Furi; take your choice from Aroleid, Silvana, Farmer Hause, Furi, Simi's, Zum See, and Blatten.

Zermatt should also be flagged as one of the best resorts in the world for nonskiers. A friend who visited the village with me and a group of avid skiers not only refused to learn to ski, but maintained that he had enjoyed "the time of his life" simply exploring the snowy footpaths, admiring the scenery, sampling the lower mountain restaurants, wandering through "old Zermatt" (a narrow street full of rustic chalets), visiting the shops and tearooms, the truly fascinating museum, and even the sad but enthralling graveyard, packed with the bodies of mainly young climbers who have perished both on the Matterhorn and other nearby peaks.

Once visited, Zermatt and its magical mountain are never forgotten and almost invariably revisited. And, strangely, no matter how many times you return, the Matterhorn always astounds you, just as it did Whymper all those years ago.

RESORT	ZERMATT
GETTING THERE:	Zürich to Zermatt: 250km (155 miles); Geneva to Zermatt: 230km (140 miles); Châtillon to Cervinia: 27km (17 miles). Regular bus services from station. Cannot reach Zermatt by car; motorists must park a little down valley at Täsch.
HEIGHT:	Zermatt: 1620–3820m (5320–12,530ft) Cervinia: 2050–3460m (6730–11,350ft)
NO. OF LIFTS:	74 (including Cervinia)
TYPES OF PISTES:	33% beg, 41% inter, 26% adv.
MAIN ADVANTAGES:	Beautiful scenery; traditional Alpine village; large selection of restaurants; car-free; linked to Cervinia.
DRAWBACKS:	Spread-out ski area; accommodations can be far from slopes. Purpose-built village in Cervinia unattractive.

OPPOSITE It's enough to make you leap for joy – the Matterhorn seems to tilt a bow to this courageous off-piste enthusiast.

interdit - not permitted - verboten
WC
SERVICE
KEEP ON
TOBLERONE
POLO SPORT

VERBIER

VALAIS, SWITZERLAND

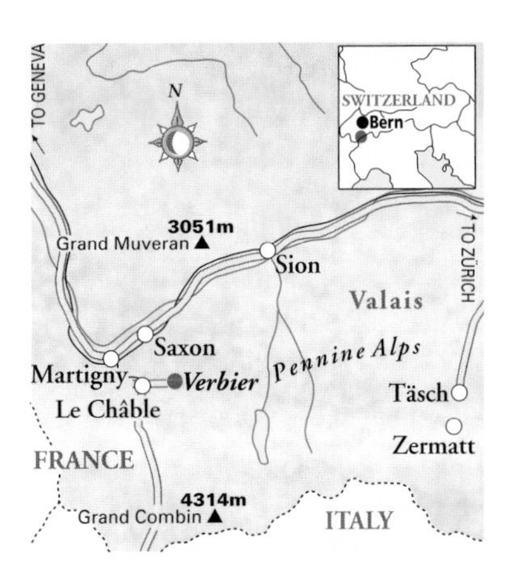

AS PEACE RETURNED TO EUROPE AFTER WORLD War II, an exciting new ski resort was just beginning to take root above the summer pastures of the Val de Bagnes in the Valais. One of the sunniest parts of Switzerland, the area's dry climate and minimal fog levels contributed to a great biological and therapeutic environment, and in 1945, just 27 people lived year-round in a hamlet that would mushroom into a ski area with 1000 chalets. Just over 160km (100 miles) from Geneva, Verbier did not last long as a "best-kept secret." A year later, the first lift was installed and there was no going back.

The "Funiluge" – a sleigh big enough to carry 12 people – was powered by a combustion engine and had to be started by hand. A cable was attached to a tree and the contraption hauled skiers up 200m (600ft). Sometimes it tipped them over into the snow. From such inauspicious beginnings grew one of the greatest ski resorts in the world, with more than 100 lifts and over 400km (250 miles) of pistes spread across four valleys, and a million visitors each year.

There are many ski areas around the world where I would be happy to show friends the ropes, if not ski under them. Verbier, however, is not one of them. After numerous visits, I still find the sheer variety of runs in various directions bewildering. Like a taxi driver trying to acquire "the knowledge" in London's myriad streets, I feel I am only halfway to passing my exams. Not only is Verbier's own network of pistes in the Val de Bagnes vast; it is also part of a much larger, four-valley system guaranteed to keep skiers and boarders entertained for as many weeks as they might have to spare.

LEFT A quick lunch. There's just too much good skiing in Verbier to waste valuable time, and the race will soon be on to get to the bottom of the Jumbo cable car for yet another ride to some of the best slopes in the Swiss Alps.

TOP On top of the world – if you ever manage to ski from the top of Mont-Fort to Le Chable, you will have accomplished a vertical drop of 2500m (8000ft).

Verbier is not ideal for beginners, but for everyone else it provides a veritable feast – especially hard-core skiers from all over the world who regard the skiing and boarding here "to die for." Unfortunately, if they ignore avalanche warnings or slip under a rope, they occasionally do. Verbier is not a place in which to be casual about safety.

Cruising? Take your pick. Particularly from the assortment of lifts around Attelas, Ruinettes, and Lac de Vaux. Gentle skiing below the trees in poor visibility? Drift down to La Tzoumaz. Bumps? They are hard to avoid on such thigh-burning descents as Gentianes to Tortin, or from the top of the Mont-Fort glacier that, at 3300m (11,000ft), is the highest point in the resort. There are wonderful views of countless peaks from the top, including the Matterhorn and Mont Blanc. Off-piste? There is more off than on. The choices are boundless. An instructor or guide is highly desirable. Heliskiing? There are some excellent options in Verbier.

RESORT	VERBIER
GETTING THERE:	Zürich: 300km (185 miles); Geneva: 160km (100 miles); Martigny: 30km (20 miles). Rail and bus services available from Geneva, Zürich and Martigny. Train station at Le Châble: 8km (5 miles).
HEIGHT:	1500–3330m (4920–10,930ft)
NO. OF LIFTS:	95 in entire ski area.
TYPES OF PISTES:	33% beg, 42% inter, 25% adv.
MAIN ADVANTAGES:	Large linked ski area, extensive off-piste; attractive town; lively nightlife.
DRAWBACKS:	Quite expensive; ski run back to resort can be busy; overcrowded pistes in certain areas.

ABOVE Downtown Verbier looks serene by night, but the local bars will be rocking! Yet somehow, most revelers will still manage to be back on the slopes early the next day.

Across the valley lies Mayens-de-Bruson, to which many Verbier locals retreat in an attempt to escape the crowds on good powder days. Attelas is the starting point to reach the legendary Mont-Gelé, with its experts-only front face, but a powder skier's joy on its much more benign backside.

Stairway To Heaven – a short sharp climb not far from the top of the Jumbo cable car at the Col des Gentianes – brings skiers and riders to several easy and enjoyable powder fields. Perhaps the ultimate is the back of Mont-Fort, where you can choose from couloirs of varying severity, none of which should be attempted without a guide.

The best way to cruise all day is simply to take the Four Valleys tour, or a section of it, although there is in fact nothing simple about it. Until Verbier produces a skier- and boarder-friendly Four Valleys map, which tallies with good signposting on the pistes, there is bound to be a certain amount of trial and error involved. Skiers and snowboarders uncertain about the rather brutal bump run can take the cable car down to Tortin. From here a gentle itinerary takes you to Veysonnaz – with perhaps a little lunch at the Igloo, at the bottom of the exhilarating Piste de L'Ours – via Siviez and Thyon. With blue skies, good snow, and a little warmth, it makes for a picturesque but relatively undemanding day's excursion.

ST. MORITZ

GRAUBÜNDEN, SWITZERLAND

ST. MORITZ IS PERHAPS THE MOST FAMOUS WINTER sports resort in the world. Even its name is copyrighted. While the town – named after St. Mauritius, a third-century Theban commander massacred for refusing to persecute Christians – is today very much the haunt of the jet set, this has not always been the case. In 1841, the French writer Rodolphe Topfer described the locals, a touch unflatteringly, as "a grotesque mixture of hardy peasants, idle gentry, tipplers, and makers of cheese!"

St. Moritz is, in a sense, where it all started – or at least where the idea of winter sports vacations first caught on. Legend has it that it was the celebrated "Badrutt wager" in 1864 that prompted the inspirational notion that a vacation in a "winter wonderland" could be fun and invigorating.

Johannes Badrutt, the owner of the Kulm Hotel, still the most venerable establishment in St. Moritz, approached a party of British clients on the point of returning after a summer in the mountains. The story goes that Badrutt put it to them like this: "It is true that winter is just around the corner. But do you know that the winter here is much more pleasant and a good deal less cold than in London? Do you realize that on sunny days it is so warm that we go about in shirtsleeves?" Then came the famous invitation, "I would like to offer you the chance of verifying my statement for yourselves," he said. "This winter you shall be my guests at the Kulm. You will not pay for your stay." If they didn't enjoy winter in St. Moritz, he even offered to pay their traveling expenses back to England. Needless to say, they returned to the resort and remained for the entire winter. An entry in the Kulm

TOP A swarm of Santas at a Christmas festival in St. Moritz. What present do you give a bearded man in red who has everything? Goggles seem to be the answer – they certainly help when you're driving a sleigh.

RIGHT High on the north-facing slopes of Corvatsch, the highest and most challenging of the three main St. Moritz ski areas. There are good off-piste opportunities for skiers and snowboarders from the summit, and a network of high intermediate runs.

Pingo - Bar
Rhäzünser
rivella

visitors' book records: "Far from finding it cold, the heat of the sun was so intense at times that sunshades were indispensable. The brilliance of the sun, the intensity of the sky and the clarity of the atmosphere quite surprised us."

The rest, as they say, is history. Two Winter Olympics and three Alpine Ski Championships later, with another scheduled for 2003, St. Moritz is the aspirational European ski resort. Helped by its idyllic location, overlooking a big, beautiful frozen lake, St. Moritz is famous for all kinds of other sports: skating, curling, horseracing, polo, ice cricket, golf, and even ski-jöring (being towed on skis behind a racehorse – half jockey, half skier). Then there is the Olympic bob run (easy – just let the driver steer and the brakeman brake while you cower and shut your eyes) and the world-famous Cresta toboggan run (very difficult – a remarkably brave solo effort with eyes wide open!), which ends in the grounds of the very same Kulm Hotel where Badrutt made his famous wager.

There are three main ski areas, all very different in character, and all spread out, plus a handful of small satellite areas thrown in. The most sensible area with which to start is the resort's own "backyard" – Corviglia. These local slopes are usually sunny, and sufficiently extensive to keep most skiers and boarders busy for a week. There is nothing very startling about the resort's original slopes here, but there are some quite steep and scenic runs down from the highest point at Piz Nair (3000m; 10,000ft). Skiers and boarders in search of challenging slopes should try the long black run from the top of the funicular at Corviglia (2486m; 8157ft) all the way down to Chantarella, where they can quickly hop back onto the funicular's second stage. Another good long black run takes you from Las Trais Fluors back to Marguns.

Elsewhere, the skiing tends to be bright, breezy, and uncomplicated. Things get somewhat tougher across the valley at Corvatsch, where a large area unfolds along quite steep terrain between Murtél and Furtschellas. The scenery here is so striking that Werner Braun, an old photographer friend of mine from Jerusalem, once gazed out across the valley and uttered, "Look how beautiful it is – what a fool Moses was not to come to St. Moritz instead of Israel!"

Most of the skiing around Murtél (2702m; 8865ft) consists of moderately difficult red runs. These link – via easier blues – with more difficult skiing as you move down the valley to Furtschellas, where at least half the pistes are black. An exhilarating long black run, from Giand Alva below Murtél, comes all the way down to St. Moritz Bad.

There is spectacular skiing in the neighboring resort of Pontresina, a charming, sedate, old-world town with hotel architecture that bears an indefinable Victorian Swiss quality. Sleepy Pontresina is the gateway to Lagalb and Diavolezza. At almost 3000m (10,000ft), Lagalb is good for a few runs down its rather bleak, windswept slopes, which include a classic black run from top to bottom. Apart from some good off-piste on the lower slopes, Diavolezza has some of the most magnificent scenery in the Engadine, with commanding views of the spectacular Diavolezza glacier and the chance to ski the extraordinarily beautiful run down to Morteratsch along the glacier's edge. The descent is easy, but the vista is magnificent. Moses would surely have been even more impressed with this view than the one from Corvatsch.

RESORT	ST MORITZ
GETTING THERE:	Munich: 300km (185 miles); Zürich: 210km (130 miles); Milan: 200km (120 miles); Samedan, St. Moritz airport: 9km (5 miles). Rail and bus services from Zürich. Glacier Express train from Zermatt. Train station in resort.
HEIGHT:	1820–3060m (5970–10,040ft)
NO. OF LIFTS:	St Moritz: 23; Engadine area: 60
TYPES OF PISTES:	10% beg, 70% inter, 20% adv.
MAIN ADVANTAGES:	Good snow record; snow-making facilities; wide choice of winter sports available; suitable for nonskiers.
DRAWBACKS:	Lifts very busy at peak times; limited number of beginner slopes; difficult road access; long overland transfers.

LEFT The Pingo-Bar igloo at the middle station of Murtél at Corvatsch is a popular place to hang out and catch a little sun. Novices can marvel at the scenery from some of the most challenging slopes on the St. Moritz circuit even if their ski technique doesn't always do them justice.

DAVOS & KLOSTERS

GRAUBÜNDEN, SWITZERLAND

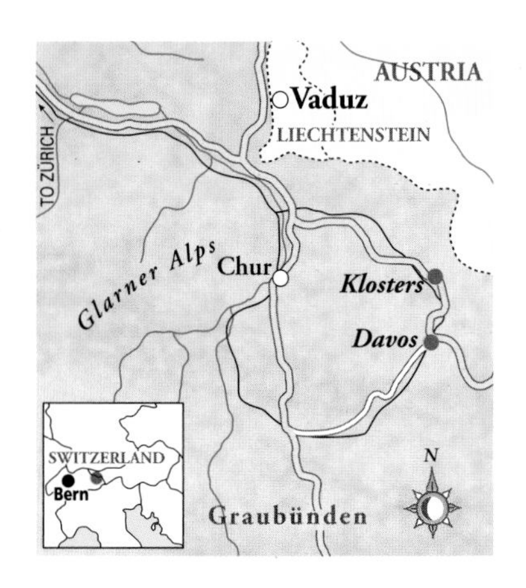

IT WAS PERHAPS THE BRITISH – AND PARTICULARLY the English – who contributed most substantially to the rather eccentric notion of winter sports. As the 20th century unfolded, they were romping in the snow and soaking up the winter sun all over Switzerland, tobogganing in St. Moritz, coining the idea of "Downhill Only" after commandeering the mountain railroad to the slopes in Wengen, and, thanks to Sir Arnold Lunn, busily setting out the first modern slalom course at Mürren. But Davos should certainly not be forgotten in the annals of ski pioneering. Indeed, the *Good Skiing and Snowboarding Guide* maintains that it is "the European birthplace of downhill skiing."

Davos, which shares much of its vast skiing area with the much more charming resort of chalet-rich Klosters (the Prince of Wales' pet resort), claims to be the highest town in Europe and is definitely much more urban than chocolate-box. It extends for some 4km (2.5 miles) between Davos Dorf and Davos Platz, and many of the hotels are former sanatoriums.

It was the medical fashion toward the end of the 19th century for people stricken with tuberculosis to come to the mountains to try to improve their health. Among them was the wife of a rather unlikely ski pioneer, Sir Arthur Conan Doyle. Setting out to make a tour "on ski" over the Maienfeld Furka Pass down to Arosa, the creator of Sherlock Holmes became the first Englishman to embark on such an adventure and at once something of a fanatic. His account of that early journey, reported in *Strand* magazine in 1894, still rings true in the 21st century and bears retelling.

TOP The ultimate ski jump. Paragliding – seriously off-piste! – is another way one can enjoy the magnificent Gotschnawang glacier and the surrounding scenery.

RIGHT The impressive lift station and restaurant at the top of the Jakobshorn offers superb views all the way across to the Bernese and Valais Alps.

RESTAURANT JAKOBS HORN
DAVOS

"Skis," Conan Doyle concluded, "are the most capricious things upon earth. One day, you cannot go wrong with them. On another, with the same weather and the same snow, you cannot go right. You have just time to say, 'What a lovely view is this!' when you find yourself standing on your two shoulder blades with your 'skis' tied tightly round your neck." He concluded, "I am convinced that the time will come when hundreds of Englishmen will come to Switzerland for the 'ski'ing season."

The first pair of skis at Davos-Klosters arrived from Norway, brought by a former patient at a TB clinic. The celebrated Parsenn Derby race – along the slopes of the Parsenn that Davos shares with Klosters – was held for the first time in 1924. It is claimed that the world's first tow lift was installed here by a young German engineer named Gerhard Müller, with the help of a rope and some motorcycle parts. Then, in 1931, came the first funicular built specifically for skiers, up to the Weissfluhjoch, gateway to the sweeping trails of the Parsenn, which until then had taken hours to reach on foot. Three years later, Erick Constam built the world's first real drag lift.

Today the Davos-Klosters region has numerous skiing and boarding permutations although, like St. Moritz, some are inconveniently spread out. But there are few resorts in the Alps with quite such a panorama of peaks. Wherever you wander the horizon seems to be pierced by jagged, snow-covered "horns" – Schwartzhorn, Bocktenhorn, Wisshorn, Scalettahorn, to name but a few – most of them well over 3000m (10,000ft).

The extensive Parsenn area, with exceptionally long runs going all the way down to Serneus and Kublis, is the key to the heart of Davos-Klosters skiing. Across the valley lies the Pischa, along with two other autonomous areas, Jakobshorn (a favorite with snowboarders) and Rinerhorn (wonderful off-piste off the back in good snow). Madrisa is a sunny, mainly lower-intermediate area above Klosters Dorf, although it does have two quite tough black runs down to the valley floor. The area is also an important gateway for ski-touring expeditions across the border into Austria. The Prince of Wales, who has enjoyed the long run down to Gargellan more than once, was often greeted by the director of the local lift company with a "black widow" – kirsch-flavored coffee with an abundance of cream.

RESORT	DAVOS & KLOSTERS
Getting There:	Zürich: 150km (95 miles). Bus and rail services available from Zürich. Train station in Davos Dorf. Only 30 mins from Davos to Klosters.
Height:	Davos: 1560–2840m (5120–9320ft) Klosters: 1200–2840m (3940–9320ft)
No. of Lifts:	Davos-Klosters: 54
Types of Pistes:	Davos: 30% beg, 50% inter, 20% adv. Klosters: 30% beg, 40% inter, 30% adv.
Main Advantages:	Large ski area; easily accessible off-piste; tree skiing; suitable for nonskiers.
Drawbacks:	Davos town is long and spread out, lacking Alpine atmosphere; quiet nightlife in Klosters; limited snow making.

Some of the most interesting skiing can be found on the runs that link Davos with Klosters, most famously the off-piste avalanche slope, the Gotschnawang, or "Wang." In 1988, Prince Charles came close to being swept away by an avalanche here. His entourage was not so lucky: Major Hugh Lyndsay was killed and Mrs. Patti Palmer-Tomkinson badly injured.

A less daunting run down to Klosters – though in many ways even more challenging – is Drostobel, for which skiers need lightning reflexes. Altogether there are 320km (200 miles) of skiing in the Davos and Klosters area, served by well over 50 lifts. In such an extensive region, the chance of finding yourself sharing a lift with the Prince of Wales is slim.

OPPOSITE The Swiss village of Klosters, the Prince of Wales' favorite skiing haunt, is in marked contrast to the neighboring town of Davos with which it shares its extensive slopes.
ABOVE With its fun park, half-pipe and boarder-cross course, the Jakobshorn has become the most popular snowboarders' mountain in the Davos area.

ANDERMATT

URI, SWITZERLAND

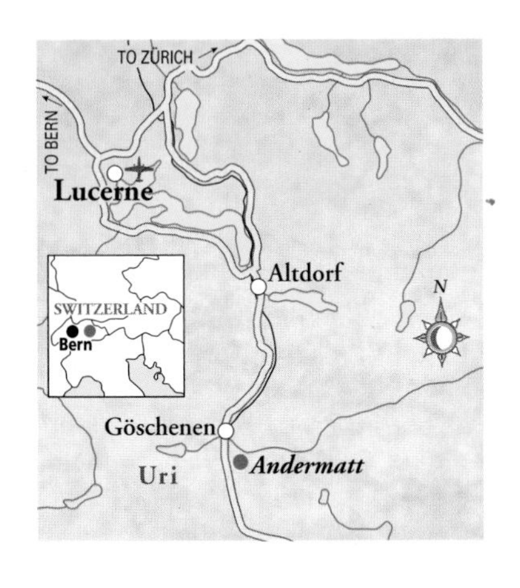

SOME EIGHT CENTURIES AGO, IN THE LITTLE-KNOWN canton of Uri, Andermatt (1444m; 4738ft) emerged from obscurity when the Teufel bridge was built and the community became a gateway between southern Germany and northern Italy. The cobblestoned village is dotted with wooden buildings and, less appealingly, the odd army barracks that speak of the Andermatt of a generation ago, when it basked in glory as a prime destination for postwar winter vacations. Gradually, however, the Swiss army (which has been associated with the resort for over a century) took over the area for the training of Alpine troops, and Andermatt is presently a far cry from the popular haunt it once was.

Today, this enigmatic and challenging resort qualifies as a kind of "lost world" of the Swiss Alps. While some still describe it as being "at the crossroads of the Alps," others argue that because Andermatt was "underpassed" by the Gotthard road tunnel in 1980, it is an Alpine dead end in winter when the natural access is considerably restricted. Family skiers have become scarce and it is now largely the domain of off-piste specialists prepared to hike up on "skins" (strips of imitation sealskin strapped to the underside of skis for better grip going uphill) in order to reach untracked snow and challenging couloirs.

From the skiing and snowboarding cognoscenti's point of view, Andermatt's comparative isolation has somewhat enhanced its reputation as a much-revered arena where individuals can pit their skills and strength against the considerable challenges the mountain offers.

TOP Although the Swiss Army has all but comandeered the once bustling ski resort of Andermatt, those in the know still come to enjoy its exceptional slopes.

RIGHT Silent night in the bleak midwinter – this church provides a bright spectacle as all remains calm in the Swiss mountain village of the remote Ursen Valley, at the "crossroads of the Alps."

Like most great resorts, Andermatt has a "magic" mountain that has made its skiing legendary – the magnificent Gemsstock (2963m; 9722ft). There is only one way up: the two-stage cable car. From the top there are various ways down, none of them easy and some sufficiently tricky to require a guide. There is also a breathtaking view, providing the summit is not blanketed in mist. Andermatt is close to the junction of four Alpine passes: Grimsel, Susten, and Oberalp, as well as the St. Gotthard. You can gaze down straight from your eyrie into three separate cantons – Graubünden, Ticino, and Valais – eliciting the proud local boast that in a single day you can eat ossobuco Ticinese, raclette with Valaisian bread, and barley soup from the Grisons.

Although the overall vertical drop is just over 1500m (5000ft), and the runs are long as well as steep, the most interesting part of the mountain is formed by the two vast bowls that dominate the front face of the Gemsstock: almost 750m (2500ft) of classic off-piste terrain. Snow is virtually guaranteed on the Gemsstock's St. Anna glacier.

Boarders and free riders come into their own on the nearby Winterhorn, which rises to 2660m (8730ft) above neighboring Hospental. There are, however, more gentle slopes at the Nätschen/Gütsch area with further skiing nearby at Realp. Between them, these resorts have 34 lifts and more than 160km (100 miles) of pistes. The Gotthard Oberalp lift pass also includes the resorts of Sedrun and Disentis.

One of the resort's most testing descents is named after Bernhard Russi, the Sapporo Olympic downhill gold medalist, better known these days as the designer of many Olympic downhills. Russi describes the 4km (2½-mile) descent thus: "This is my favorite run, and one of the most beautiful descents in the Alps. For carving skiers, it's sensational."

RESORT	ANDERMATT
GETTING THERE:	Bern: 180km (110 miles); Zürich: 120km (75 miles); Lucerne: 60km (35 miles). Train station in Göschenen 6km (4 miles). Shuttle services from Zürich and Bern airports and Göschenen train station.
HEIGHT:	1450–2960m (4760–9710ft)
NO. OF LIFTS:	9 in Andermatt; 34 in area
TYPES OF PISTES:	44% beg, 28% inter, 28% adv.
MAIN ADVANTAGES:	Traditional village; friendly resort; north-facing slopes; abundant snowfall.
DRAWBACKS:	Two separate ski areas; ski lifts could be more efficient; Gemsstock not ideal for beginners.

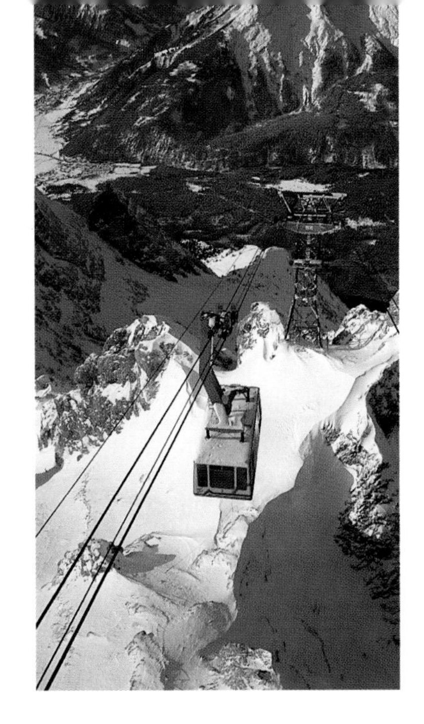

Garmisch-Partenkirchen

BAVARIA, GERMANY

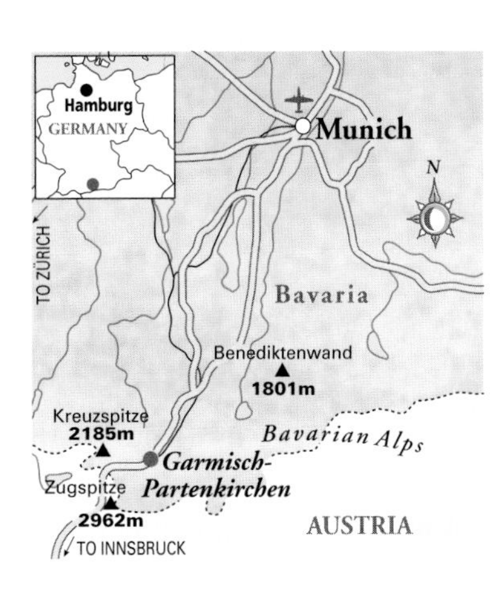

WHAT WOULD THE AMERICANS – WHO HAVE FOR years attempted to re-create Bavarian/Tyrolean charm in the Rockies – not give to have a ski resort packed with old-world Alpine architecture like Garmisch-Partenkirchen? It doesn't get any more Bavarian or charming than these twin towns – the scenery, crowned by the mighty Zugspitze (2964m; 9725ft), which lies partly in Germany and partly in Austria, is inspirational. Indeed, it was probably the American love affair with Garmisch that inspired the town planners at Vail, Colorado, to build a ski resort that was once unkindly dubbed a "plastic Bavaria." At Leavenworth, near the resort of Stevens Pass in Washington State, they built an entire town in Bavarian style. The Canadians had a similar idea when they built the eccentric neo-Bavarian town center at Kimberley in British Columbia. To make the resort more authentic they even imported a genuine German restaurant; the Old Bauernhaus, a 400-year-old structure, was shipped over in sections and re-erected. Nothing plastic about that.

In a sense, the Americans do have a slice of genuine Bavaria. At the end of the last war, American forces had formed such an attachment to the place that they did not want to leave. And many didn't. The U.S. Army built a European recreation center here, and GI ski enthusiasts were among the first to test the prototype ski safety bindings developed by the now well-known Hannes Marker. To this day, American skiers visit Garmisch in the thousands. There are four American-owned hotels, and there's even a private mini-resort, complete with its own ski hill and T-bar, reserved for U.S. Army and NATO forces.

TOP The cable car takes you to the top of the Zugspitze, but since it is unthinkable for recreational skiers to ski down, you need another cable car to descend to the slopes.

LEFT When North American ski resorts attempted to recapture the flavor of the Alps, they were sometimes unkindly dismissed as a "plastic Bavaria." This is the real thing: Garmisch has medieval origins, and Partenkirchen dates back to 15 B.C.

LEFT Snowy rooftops add to the colorful charm of Garmisch. Many of the buildings here and in Partenkirchen are beautifully decorated with colorful *luftmalerei* frescoes.

Garmisch and Partenkirchen are spread out beneath a great horseshoe of jagged peaks formed by the Wettersteingebirge and Ammergauer mountain ranges. Partenkirchen, an ancient Roman settlement dating back to 15 B.C., and Garmisch, with its slightly more recent medieval roots, became an "item" at Hitler's insistence to host the 1936 Winter Olympics. The high-walled Olympic stadium, below the ski jumps, looks much the same as it did 65 years ago. The original observation towers are still there. One, painted dark green, bears an unsettling resemblance to a wartime lookout tower – in stark contrast to the delightful old buildings in the twin towns, many of which have colorful *luftmalerei* frescos on their exterior walls. Indeed, Germany's principal ski area is such a joy to behold, from top to bottom, that visitors can scarcely fail to be of good cheer, except perhaps in a total whiteout. The scenery is so spectacular that it almost does not matter that the skiing is not quite premier league, although there are certainly some challenging slopes, particularly the infamous Kandahar downhill.

One of the drawbacks of the resort is that the various ski areas are fragmented. Although Garmisch is as famous for its glacial slopes on the flanks of the Zugspitze as it is for its annual World Cup races, the two are completely separate entities. The races are held not on the Zugspitze itself, but lower down on the wooded slopes of Kreuzeck. There are three ways of reaching the Zugspitze slopes, adding a little variety to the prospect of the longish journey to the glacier. From Garmisch itself there is a choice between cable car and cog railroad. Unless you are in a rush to reach the slopes, the railroad, with a short cable car ride at the end of the trip, is more fun. The cable car takes you to the very top of the Zugspitze, but since it is absolutely unthinkable (to all but the most extreme skiers) to ski down to the glacier, it is necessary to take another cable car down to the slopes on the Zugspitze Platt.

On the Austrian side, the glacier can also be reached from the Tyrolean resort of Ehrwald, which helps create all kinds of skiing possibilities. The so-called "Happy Card" enables skiers and boarders to visit six resorts in the region: Garmisch-Partenkirchen's own portfolio of areas (the Zugspitze glacier plateau, Alpspitze-Kreuzeck-Hausberg, and Wank-Eckbauer) plus the Austrian resorts of Seefeld, Mittenwald, and the "Schneearena Tiroler Zugspitze," which includes Ehrwald and Lermoos. There is a particularly challenging descent, which should be undertaken only with a guide, from the top of the Zugspitze down to Ehrwald.

Garmisch and Partenkirchen are liberally dotted with cozy, rustic *stuben* (bars) and welcoming tearooms, many of them quite ancient. At the 16th-century Clausings-Posthotel, you can dine in the ornate Postüberl with iconic pictures spread across the walls and post horns hanging from the ceiling. In its heyday as a staging post, the hotel and its "stablemate" – the Posthotel in Partenkirchen – could accommodate hundreds of horses. Today they focus on tourists.

RESORT	GARMISCH-PARTENKIRCHEN
GETTING THERE:	Zürich: 310km (190 miles); Munich: 120km (75 miles); Innsbruck: 60km (35 miles). Rail and bus services available from Munich and Innsbruck. Train station at Garmisch-Partenkirchen.
HEIGHT:	740–2830m (2430–9290ft)
NO. OF LIFTS:	28
TYPES OF PISTES:	23% beg, 66% inter, 11% adv.
MAIN ADVANTAGES:	High-altitude skiing; picturesque Alpine villages.
DRAWBACKS:	Six resorts but fragmented ski areas.

CORTINA D'AMPEZZO

VENETO, ITALY

THE DOLOMITES ARE PART OF THE ALPS – AND YET supremely different. As different as chalk from cheese, or in their case, limestone from granite. Many have tried to describe them, some with moderate success, but the only real way to appreciate their extraordinary beauty is to see them with your own eyes. There is a famous scene in Edmond Rostand's *Cyrano de Bergerac*, in which the hero describes his long nose in a variety of ways. With the help of writers Dana Facaros and Michael Pauls in the *Cadogan Guide to Italy*, one can attempt something similar with the Dolomites.

Hence, the scientific take: "The Dolomites are formed of calcium magnesium carbonate with a covering of malleable calcite. At sunset they turn pink. This dramatic effect is caused by porphyry, a reddish purple rock of large feldspar crystals embedded in the limestone." The historic: "Born as massive corals in the primordial ocean, and heaved up from the seabed 60 million years ago, tempests and blizzards over the eons have whittled away the malleable calcite to form an extraordinary landscape." The poetic: "Otherworldly and majestic peaks claw and scratch at the sky, a petrified tempest of jagged needles, pinnacles, and sheer cliffs." The biographical: "These most romantic of mountains were named after a wandering French mineralogist with a fantastic name: Déodat Sylvain Guy Tancrède de Gratet de Dolomieu."

Now, into this exotic mix plant the vibrant town of Cortina d'Ampezzo, Italy's most affluent, fashionable, fur-coated, mobile phone-carrying ski destination, and you can sense why this scenic resort is so popular. Rich Italians, in particular, are estimated to make up some 90 percent of the clientele.

TOP Skiing is the fourth most popular pastime at Cortina, after sunbathing – here at the Refugio Ra Valles Restaurant – lunching, and après-ski, which can start early in the afternoon.

RIGHT We have liftoff – and here's hoping for a happy landing. Most recreational skiers are content to ski around the Dolomites, but for those in search of excitement – and some big air – there's only one way to go and that's straight down.

Cortina, just two hours by road from Venice, is almost entirely surrounded by a vast amphitheater of stirring mountain peaks: Le Tofane, Cristallo, Sorapis (all well over 3000m; 10,000ft), Pomagagnon, Croda da Lago, Averau, and the Cinque Torri. Splendid as it is, this arrangement, as with St. Moritz and Davos in Switzerland, results in the various ski areas being rather spread out, which in turn means having to deliberate each morning about which slopes you wish to visit. Many Italians will have probably already made up their minds: all but the "serious" skiers and snowboarders will head for the sunniest lunch spots as early as possible, leaving the various slopes and wide-open spaces free for everyone else. After lunch, the highlight of the day, there may be a similar situation since Cortina's après-ski starts early and sometimes consists of just the après – a considerable proportion of Cortina's visitors rarely bother to ski. It helps that most of the mountain restaurants have fabulous views.

The nearest (and highest) slopes to the traffic-free town center are at the popular Tofane area, linked with a wonderful network of beginner slopes at Socrepes. On the other side of the valley, also accessed by cable car, are two more linked areas, Staunies and Faloria. The smaller area of Cinque Torri is uncrowded and enjoys terrific views and exhilarating cruising. Cortina, which hosted the Winter Olympics in 1956, has its fair share of challenges: down the steep, quite narrow chute from the top of Cristallo at Forcella Staunies, for example, or the long black down to the bottom of the Rumerlo chair from the Ra Valles bowl. But the vast proportion of runs are ideal for intermediates, and some of them are wonderfully long.

After skiing, the focus of attention for people watchers is the early evening *passeggiata* (stroll) along the pedestrianized Corso Italia. The street is soon packed with wealthy, fur- and jewelry-clad visitors from Milan and Venice wandering in and out of antique shops, designer boutiques, assorted bars, and even the co-op, which in Cortina has marble floors and sells designer clothes. I once traipsed up and down this cobblestoned street searching for something readily available in just about every other ski resort in the world: a hat bearing the name of the resort on it as a souvenir for a friend. I failed to find one – even at the co-op, which treated my request with dignified disdain.

You should attempt to spare a day of your vacation in Cortina to try the celebrated Sella Ronda, a grand circular tour around the spectacular peaks of the Gruppo Sella. It is a great day's outing; the tour, approximately 40km (25 miles), takes you through four regions and several picturesque towns and villages, including Colfosco, Corvara, Arabba (which has some of the more challenging skiing), and Canazei. With a fair amount of undemanding skiing and some flattish sections, the tour is perhaps not always ideal for snowboarders. For skiers and snowboarders interested in serious exploration, there is a unique lift ticket, the Dolomiti Superski pass, which covers an astonishing 1200km (750 miles) of pistes served by 460 ski lifts. They are not linked, of course, so to do them justice, you will definitely need a car.

LEFT Spot the skiers. The immense limestone peaks of the Dolomites that dwarf these skiers also provide a breathtaking backdrop to every outing.

RIGHT Le Tofane, Cortina's highest area, mirrored here in an Alpine lake. You must leave your skis behind to reach the summit, however: the top of Le Tofane is for sunbathers and sightseers only.

RESORT	CORTINA D'AMPEZZO
GETTING THERE:	Venice: 160km (100 miles); Innsbruck: 160km (100 miles). Train services from Calalzo di Cadore and Dobbiaco: 30km (20 miles).
HEIGHT:	1220–3240m (4000–10,630ft)
NO. OF LIFTS:	37
TYPES OF PISTES:	47% beg, 43% inter, 10% adv.
MAIN ADVANTAGES:	Stunning scenery; lively atmosphere; suitable for non-skiers; great mountain restaurants.
DRAWBACKS:	Spread-out additional ski areas. Very crowded during Italian holidays. Little to offer experts.

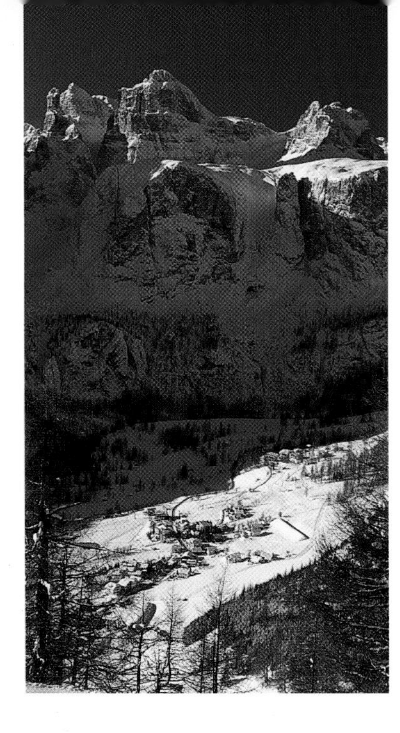

SELVA & VAL GARDENA

TRENTINO-ALTO ADIGE, ITALY

AS THE DOLOMITES NEAR SELVA CATCH THE DYING rays of the sun, the appropriate sentiment in the Ladin dialect might be *"I ie sta n bel di"* (It has been a beautiful day). Like its neighbor Cortina, Selva rejoices in spectacular dolomitic scenery; it feels as though you can almost reach out and touch the Gruppo Sella and Sassolungo, those splendid mountains that are at their most brilliant at dawn and late afternoon, when the sun's rays tint them with a sumptuous glow, splashing pink on the jagged brown crags. You can admire them all day as you circumnavigate them on skis in the famous Sella Ronda circuit. Selva, in the Val Gardena, is one of those places in Italy's South Tyrol that has a split personality: a large part of the region was annexed from the Austro-Hungarian empire by Italy after World War I. Almost invariably, these places have both an Italian and a Germanic name. Selva's alter ego, for example, is Wolkenstein. Locals speak not only Italian and German but also Ladin, a local dialect based on a form of Latin, introduced by the Romans.

This combination of cultures does much to enrich both regional cuisine and customs; at local restaurants you can order anything from *polenta con cervo* (with venison) or *con camoscio* (with chamois) to Wiener schnitzel.

The war between Austria and Italy in this part of the world was a particularly cruel one, fought high in the mountains. As many soldiers died in avalanches – often caused deliberately by the enemy – as from shells and bullets. Where you get off the chair lift at the top of the Marmolada, at

TOP Shimmering in the midday sun in the Val Badia – a bird's eye view of Colfosco, one of many picturesque towns and villages you visit during the 23km (14-mile) Sella Ronda, a delightful tour around the Gruppo Sella.

RIGHT A closer view reveals part of the quaint old town in detail, with the Dolomites rising sheer in the background. Having negotiated the Passo Gardena via Danterceppies, Colfosco is the first major town you reach after Selva.

CAPPELLA****
RESIDENCE

3342m (10,965ft) the highest peak in the Dolomites, you will find a fascinating war museum "guarded" by a World War I cannon and packed with all kinds of battle trophies and souvenirs: shell cases, helmets, grenades, and other wartime memorabilia.

Apart from a large ski area of its own with 81 lifts (including six cable cars and gondolas) serving 110km (70 miles) of local skiing, the Val Gardena (Gröden) resorts of Ortisei, Selva, and Santa Cristina provide a gateway to the celebrated Sella Ronda ski circuit. At the center of the circuit, soaring into a cornflower-blue sky, are the gigantic limestone monoliths of the Gruppo Sella. All you have to do is ski around them. This delightful and not particularly challenging tour can be achieved fairly easily in a day. Allow time for lunch and even more time to admire the splendid scenery. You can ski it in either direction, clockwise (follow the orange arrows) or counter-clockwise (green boards), from Val Gardena, Val di Fassa, Alta Badia, or Arabba. Mountain villages and towns seem to drift past you all day as you cruise effortlessly (apart from a few flat sections – snowboarders note) through the picturesque towns and villages of Colfosco, Corvara, and San Cassiano, on through the wooded slopes of Canazei, and steeper, more challenging slopes at Arabba. Try to make time for a detour to the wonderful, long, plunging runs of the Marmolada glacier.

The Val Gardena is almost 25km (16 miles) long, and it lies between Bressanone (Brixen) and Bolzano in the eastern part of South Tyrol. The Val Gardena-Alpe di Siusi resorts are divided into four main ski areas: Rasciesa-Seceda-Col Raiser, Alpe di Siusi, Danterceppies (where the first downhill race in Selva was held in 1908) and Ciampinoi-Plan de Gralba-Passo Sella-Monte Pana. Most of the almost 300 instructors claim to speak English, as well as Italian and German, and almost certainly a little Ladin.

The towering massifs create an almost primeval backdrop as skiers cruise their way around them. Yet as they progress across the Sella, Pordoi, Campolongo, and Gardena passes, they may be unaware that above them in the craggy heights are several rather more dramatic descents. The unusual shape of the Dolomites – gigantic, often near-vertical slabs of limestone – produces a dramatic contrast in the terrain. The vast majority of people ski around the Dolomites rather than down them, so the bulk of the pistes are fairly easy. The off-piste itineraries, however, are challenging – some seriously so.

One of the highlights is the Val di Mezdi, above Colfosco, a classic steep-sided gully with a fearsome-looking entrance. The only way to reach it is by cable car and then quite a long hike between towering rock walls.

LEFT Time for a breather at Seceda, Selva's local slopes. The combination of Italian and Austrian cultures here means you can order anything from polenta with venison to goulash.

The Val di Mezdi starts at around 2800m (9200ft) on the rim of a craggy, inverted archway near the summit of Sasso Pordoi, another of the towering peaks that dominate the Selva skyline. What makes it challenging is the narrowness of the entrance and the impact of the sheer dolomite walls that seem almost to enclose you. As you take the plunge, small stones fall alarmingly from the towering rock faces on either side. By the time you reach Colfosco, you will have descended over 1200m (4000ft).

The picturesque old town of Ortisei (1236m; 4055ft), the principal community and cultural center of Val Gardena, is both chic and traditional and has its own small ski area. It is linked with Selva and the Sella Ronda circuit by bus.

Val Gardena is the venue for one of the early World Cup meetings each season. The Saslonch downhill run to Santa Cristina – with its famous "camel bumps" – is the scene of the Men's Downhill on Mount Ciampinoi. Danterceppies, with its Cir run, is the location for the women's course.

Apart from its outstanding scenery, skiing, and local cuisine, Val Gardena is world famous for its woodcarving. Once known as the "valley of the woodcarvers," Gardena's products were originally carried out on foot. By 1780, they had found their way to all corners of the globe and so many trees were being used to carve statues, altars, nativity scenes, and ornaments that a decree reduced the number of carvers by half. In spite of this, more than 200 years later, the region is brimming with carvings, from baroque to modern. So far, it seems none of the craftsmen have tried carving ... carving skis!

RESORT	SELVA & VAL GARDENA
GETTING THERE:	Milan: 300km (185 miles); Venice: 190km (120 miles); Verona: 140km (85 miles). Train service from Bolzano: 40km (25 miles), Bressanone: 35km (22 miles) and Chiusa: 25km (15 miles).
HEIGHT:	1060–2520m (3480–8270ft)
NO. OF LIFTS:	81; 460 in Dolomiti Superski area
TYPES OF PISTES:	30% beg, 60% inter, 10% adv.
MAIN ADVANTAGES:	Beautiful, unique Dolomite scenery; excellent snow-making and grooming; large number of new lifts.
DRAWBACKS:	Erratic snow record; limited advanced level slopes.

RIGHT The hauntingly majestic Sassolungo, crowning glory of the Selva/Wolkenstein region, viewed from the Gruppo Sella.

ÅRE

JÄMTLAND, SWEDEN

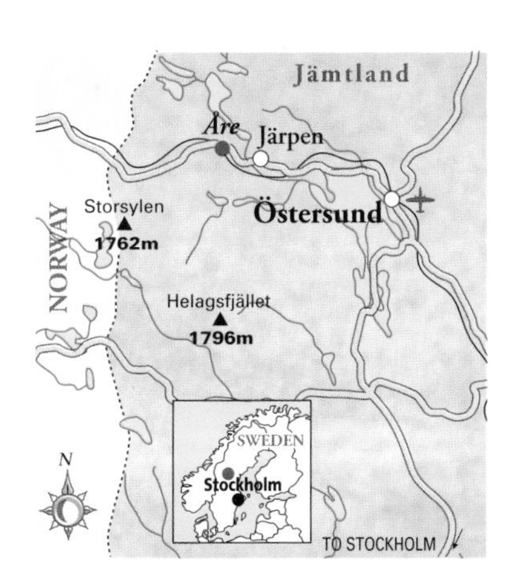

DOWNHILL SKIING IN ÅRE STARTED UNDER HEROIC but tragic circumstances. Over a bottle of *akvavit,* villagers challenged a Samisk (Lapp) woman called Zeta to ski from the top of Åreskutan, the highest peak in the Åre region, all the way down to the village. Zeta won the bet but lost her life. Arriving in the village square suffering from extreme cold, she collapsed and died. In spite of her fate, Zeta's example was followed by other local skiers, fortunately without such serious consequences. Åre's first downhill race was held in 1921 and Scandinavia's foremost ski resort now regularly hosts World Cup downhills.

Åre, short for Årefjällen, is strung out along a big frozen lake, Lake Åresjön, and is perhaps reminiscent of St. Moritz – just as vibrant but in a much more remote setting. An old brochure describes the contrast well as "the beauty and silence of the untouched wilderness alongside the pulsating entertainment of a winter sports village." It takes about an hour-and-a-quarter to drive there from Östersund, but by far the most romantic method of traveling is to make the journey by rail. A special high-speed ski-train link from Stockholm was introduced recently, with a journey time of five-and-a-half hours. It was, in fact, the arrival of the railroad in the 1880s that exposed this idyllic lake district to tourism, and skiing in particular.

Åre has an unusually varied choice of skiing; the resort is divided into four areas – Duved, Tegefjäll, Åre, and Åre Björnen – with 100km (60 miles) of groomed runs (almost 100 pistes) served by more than 44 lifts, which include Sweden's only cable car and a funicular. Two new six-seater

LEFT Who said Swedish ski areas don't get much sunshine? The Swedish flag flutters proudly on a blue-sky day while skiers and boarders take their gloves off and contemplate the view during a lunchtime break on the slopes.

TOP Who needs an artificial half-pipe when the mountain has features like the Östra Ravin? With more sky than ski, this free rider is determined to match the snowboarders.

RESORT	ÅRE
GETTING THERE:	Nearest airport, Östersund: 100km (60 miles). Regular bus service, mornings and afternoons, from Östersund to Åre. Direct trains from Stockholm and Gothenburg.
HEIGHT:	380–1270m (1250–4170ft)
NO. OF LIFTS:	44
TYPES OF PISTES:	11% beg, 79% inter, 10% adv.
MAIN ADVANTAGES:	Largest ski area in Scandinavia; many winter sports available; attractive village; great for families; lively nightlife.
DRAWBACKS:	Short days during early/midseason; can be very cold; remote resort, can be difficult to get to.

chair lifts are in the pipeline. Another small area, Edsåsdalen, lies across the lake. Although many of the slopes are easy, there are any number of challenging runs, including the Slalombacken, the Skogis run through the forest at Björnen, and, of course, the World Cup downhill course.

This far north the snow is almost invariably good, although it does get dark early in midwinter. The sun sets around 2:30 P.M. on January 1, but by early February it is after 4:00 P.M. before the sun goes down. Either way, there is night skiing and boarding at Gästrappet and Lundsrappet (with lighting so powerful you almost need sunglasses) for those who want to keep going instead of making an early start to the après-ski.

Off-piste is plentiful, including the huge Susabäckravin, a ravine much favored by free riders and snowboarders. From Åre's so-called "high area," you can hitch a ride behind a snowmobile (weather permitting) to the very top of Åreskutan, the principal mountain. This will give you a vertical drop of some 1000m (3300ft). Heliskiing at Snasahögarna is also possible. Other activities include husky and snowmobile safaris, horseback riding, ice climbing, reindeer sleigh rides, paragliding, and tobogganing. In 2000, the resort held its first gay ski festival. And introduced "snowfering" – windsurfing on snow on the frozen lake.

Duved and neighboring Tegefjäll have some delightful skiing; mainly long cruising runs, often through the trees. Both areas have good nursery slopes, too. But the focus of interest is Åre itself, with a tremendous variety of slopes. The resort has several cozy, charming, and often quite reasonably priced mountain restaurants. For something different, at the bottom of Stendalen, you are likely to find Lapps serving reindeer burgers, sandwiches, coffee, and pastries from benches in front of their *goahtes* (tepees).

The Björnen area consists mainly of good cruising through the woods. It is also the place parents with young children head for. It has a special section in the middle of the village, with a ski school and après-ski for children. Younger children can be left for the day at the Barnens Hus kindergarten.

It is after dusk, of course, that the Swedes really come into their own as a visit to either the Diplomat Ski Lodge or the Sunwing Hotel will confirm. At the Sunwing, a huge pile of ski boots outside the bar announces the commencement of Sweden's favorite alpine pastime: dancing to live bands. The village – typically alpine in a way few other Scandinavian resorts can emulate – has five discotheques, numerous bars, ski lodges, and other nightspots. The Swedes may be good skiers, but they are undeniably expert après-skiers.

TOP LEFT On a clear day you can ski forever – competitors in the 2001 Red Bull Big Air competition pause on terra firma before taking a leap of faith at Åre, Sweden's most exciting ski resort.

RIKSGRÄNSEN & NARVIK

NORRBOTTEN, SWEDEN & NORDLAND, NORWAY

THERE ARE NOT MANY RESORTS WHERE YOU FIND yourself skiing unwittingly over the wreckage of an airplane still half-buried in the permafrost. But this is one of the oddities of a visit to Riksgränsen, Sweden's most northerly ski area. As they cruise such runs as Lämmeln (Lemming), Vargtassen (Wolf's Paw), Fjällräven (Arctic Fox), and Klunken (Gulp!), most skiers and boarders will be unaware that remnants of the Junkers transport aircraft lie beneath the arctic snows covering Skrattvallen (The Laughing Wall). The German aircraft was shot down by Swedish partisans in 1941 and only two of the seven passengers and crew survived. The snow hides the wreckage for most of the year, revealing its secret only briefly each fall. Riksgränsen is so close to the Norwegian border that you can ski into Norway almost without knowing it. An important rail link between Kiruna and the Norwegian port of Narvik passes close to the Riksgränsen Hotel, where most skiers and snowboarders stay.

Riksgränsen started life just over a century ago as a railroad outpost. Huge quantities of iron ore were being mined at Kiruna and transported to Narvik. The railroad line became a vital line of supply during the war when, in spite of Sweden's declared neutrality, it allowed Germany to send troops, equipment, and stores to Narvik and use the return leg to bring wounded soldiers and prisoners of war back to Germany. The Allied fleet, suspecting that the Germans were using the iron ore to fuel their war machine, attacked Narvik. Swedish partisans attempted to sabotage the German war effort, hence the stricken Junkers beneath the Arctic snows.

TOP Which way is down? In the unlikely event of poor snow, you could always make for Nordpolen – you may think you're far north in this part of the Arctic Circle, but the North Pole is still 2420km (1500 miles) away.

RIGHT More of a leap than a laugh – this adventurous skier obviously prefers to get his air from Riksgränsen's steep-sided half-pipe than from The Laughing Wall. It's a great view from up here too, if you can look up from your landing spot long enough.

Only the eternal darkness of early winter prevents the slopes from being open right through from October until June. Because of its extreme position, on the northwestern tip of Swedish Lapland, Riksgränsen's ski season does not really get started until February when there are sufficient daylight hours. Gradually, as spring wears on, the jagged peaks, narrow fjords, and deep valleys of this hauntingly beautiful Arctic wasteland are flooded with sunlight all night. By midsummer's day, the end of the season, the sun will not have set for over a month – and will stay above the horizon for another month.

Some skiers and boarders celebrate the long summer days – particularly Midsummer Day – by heading for the slopes under the midnight sun. During my last visit I went heliskiing at 2:00 A.M. in virtually broad daylight. After such an exhilarating experience, it was difficult to get to sleep with sunshine creeping under the blinds of the Riksgränsen Hotel.

The lifts finally close on Midsummer Day, but the hotel remains open. Riksgränsen is known principally for its extensive off-piste opportunities and, unlike many resorts, lists the most important of them, such as Branten, Ravinen, and Gränsängarna, on its trail map. Riksgränsen's Gränsleden runs are actually in Norway, and Narvik is only a short trip by rail or road.

Narvik is a rather bleak Norwegian port with a modest but unexpectedly rewarding local ski hill within three minutes of the town center. A gondola and a chair lift take snow users to the shoulder of Fagernsfjellet mountain some 1000m (3300ft) above the Ofotfjord. No passing stranger could fail to stare in amazement at the glittering seascapes framed by the snow-capped mountains of the Lofoten Islands in the distance.

The self-styled "technology center" of the Arctic is in no way a resort, rather an ice-free port whose somewhat drab gray streets are shared between earnest engineering students from Narvik College and opportunistic businessmen who make a living out of supplying essentials on the outer fringes of the earth. The hotels are functionally commercial, most of the restaurants rather unappetizing, and the nightlife virtually nonexistent. The ski area consists of broad intermediate pistes, sufficiently demanding to stage a World Cup race, but not extensive enough to keep an avid cruiser occupied for more than a morning.

The real prize, the magnificent Mörkhåla (Black Hole) snow bowl, requires a half-hour ridge walk above the top lift station, skis on shoulders, feet slithering in deep snow. At the point of no return, the guide breaks the cornice with care, then cuts loose in a powder field that, for a black hole, is a taste of white magic. After supplying seemingly endless perfect turns, the terrain finally breaks up, with streams to ford and thickets to bushwhack as the shoreline approaches. In latitudes where the sun barely sets in late spring, there is no sense of urgency. No one seems to care how long it takes when they can ski to dinner as easily as lunch.

RESORT	RIKSGRÄNSEN & NARVIK
GETTING THERE:	Kiruna: 130km (80 miles); domestic flights between Stockholm and Kiruna. Taxi and bus services available. Riksgränsen to Narvik: 50km (30 miles).
HEIGHT:	Narvik: 1280m (4200ft) Riksgränsen: 520–910m (1710–2990ft)
NO. OF LIFTS:	Narvik: 5; Riksgränsen: 6
TYPES OF PISTES:	Narvik: 20% beg, 40% inter, 40% adv. Riksgränsen: 37% beg, 58% inter, 5% adv.
MAIN ADVANTAGES:	Narvik: Beautiful scenery and fjords; excellent off-piste. Riksgränsen: Summer skiing; good value heliskiing.
DRAWBACKS:	Narvik: Limited lift-served terrain; limited après-ski. Riksgränsen: Limited après-ski; very few hotels.

OPPOSITE Riksgränsen by day. Or is it by night? At midsummer it is as though the sun, having sunk toward the horizon, has a change of heart and decides not to set after all.
ABOVE High above the Ofotfjord, a lone skier tackles the off-piste run that heads straight down to the water. The Mörkhåla (Black Hole) run is the highlight of Narvik's skiing.

THE AMERICAS

WHISTLER & BLACKCOMB, LAKE LOUISE & BANFF, FERNIE
ASPEN, JACKSON HOLE, LAKE TAHOE, VAIL,
PARK CITY, SNOWBIRD & ALTA, TAOS SKI VALLEY, TELLURIDE
VALLE NEVADO, LA PARVA & EL COLORADO, PORTILLO
LAS LEÑAS, SAN CARLOS DE BARILOCHE

Just as the grass is inevitably greener on the other side, so the snow can be perceived to be lighter, whiter, and fluffier. Certainly there is a widespread belief that the snow in the American and Canadian Rockies is special. North Americans like nothing better than to visit the Alps. On the other hand, the Europeans – particularly the British – are intoxicated by the notion of skiing in the Wild West.

While European resorts are often bigger than those in North America, resorts in the Rockies are frequently better organized, better groomed, and more likely to have that essential ingredient: powder.

Moving south to the Andes, the resorts in Chile and Argentina tend to be a little less streamlined. But the friendly locals and the awe-inspiring nature of the Andes make up for this. Every visitor I have met seems to agree with me that skiing in South America is almost a spiritual experience, the like of which I have never quite felt elsewhere.

LEFT All gone to look for America... the Rockies lure skiers and snowboarders from all over the world in their quest for some of the driest, lightest powder, particularly in Colorado. Vail, the USA's biggest single ski mountain, is celebrated for its "back bowls" where powder collects and is left undisturbed.

WHISTLER & BLACKCOMB

BRITISH COLUMBIA, CANADA

A MERE 35 YEARS AGO, ON THE SITE OF THIS NOW world-famous ski area, there was virtually nothing. The blizzards caused by the moist Pacific air meeting the craggy mountaintops fell silently on what was then known as London Mountain, skied only by the occasional visitor willing to use a couple of rudimentary tows or hike up to reach the best slopes. Renamed Whistler Mountain in 1965 (after the cry of the ubiquitous western hoary marmot, or whistle pig), this area is today home to one of the most popular ski resorts in the world.

Whistler Village is an attractive, purpose-built resort with truly terrific skiing. If you believed the hype, you would think that Whistler and Blackcomb stood head and shoulders above the remainder of the North American continent. Physically at least, this happens to be true – these two magnificent mountains do have the largest vertical drop in the country, both about a mile high. And Whistler is a wonderful resort – though possibly damned with too much praise. One American ski magazine labeled it the "Number One Resort in North America" year after year, inviting scepticism. Every resort has its pros and cons and Whistler, wonderful though it is, is no exception.

One of its few snags is its low elevation. At 675m (2214ft), close to the maritime influence of the Pacific seaboard, Whistler tends to attract more than its fair share of rain. Although this nearly always results in fresh snowfalls higher up the mountain, the prospect of going out in the wet to start a day's skiing puts a slight damper on things. Avid skiers and boarders, however, will hardly give it a moment's thought; indeed, I have enjoyed some of the most wonderfully deep powder at

TOP With his own snowy vapor trail, a lone skier is airborne high above Whistler's Coastal Range, enjoying the biggest vertical drop in North America – and then some.

RIGHT One of the most exhilarating moments for an off-piste skier – bursting through a cornice, you hit zero-G for a split second and then power down the bowl at Piccolo in perfect powder.

LEFT The recently redesigned Roundhouse Lodge on Whistler Mountain offers "everything from burgers and fries to fresh pasta and Asian cuisine."

Whistler when it has been raining in the village. But for fair-weather skiers it can sometimes make the difference between having a go and not bothering. For those who do make the effort there is, by anyone's standards, a colossal amount of skiing to enjoy.

Comparisons tend to be odious but it is difficult to resist comparing Whistler, the original ski mountain, with Blackcomb, where the first trails were cut just before 1980. For years the two mountains were intense rivals until in 1997, Intrawest, the major world player in ski-resort development and owner of Blackcomb, purchased Whistler too.

RESORT	WHISTLER & BLACKCOMB
GETTING THERE:	Vancouver: 120km (75 miles). Train, bus, taxi, and limousine services available from Vancouver. Train station in Whistler Creekside. Drive from Vancouver is along the spectacularly scenic Sea to Sky Highway (99 North).
HEIGHT:	Blackcomb: 675–2280m (2210–7480ft) Whistler: 650–2180m (2130–7150ft)
NO. OF LIFTS:	33
TYPES OF PISTES:	20% beg, 55% inter, 25% adv.
MAIN ADVANTAGES:	Excellent choice of restaurants; lively après-ski; wide range of skiing.
DRAWBACKS:	Proximity to coast can cause heavy rain at resort level.

Superficially, the two mountains are quite similar. Each has more than 100 trails, many of them long cruising runs through pine forests. Both mountains are highly rated by snowboarders. But Whistler has more bowls – Symphony, Glacier, Whistler, Harmony, and West Bowls – while Blackcomb has glaciers – Blackcomb and Horstman – and more couloirs, such as Couloir Extreme and Pakalolo. Runs like this are tough and unnerving in difficult conditions, but exhilarating in deep snow.

Toward the bottom of Extreme, in a golden triangle formed by two quad chairs – the Glacier Express and the Jersey Cream Express – lies a magnificent collection of chutes and gullies spread across the mountain. In fresh snow, single black diamond runs like The Bite, Staircase, and Blowdown can provide a half-day's entertainment on their own. The so-called "Great Beyond" is another big Blackcomb attraction for adventurous skiers. Runs like Blow Hole, Garnet, Diamond, and Ruby Bowls are accessed by picking your way up a frozen staircase called Spanky's Ladder, accessible from the top of the Glacier Express quad.

The key to Whistler's celebrated bowl skiing is two lifts: the old Peak triple chair and the much more recently installed Harmony Express quad. The bowls will keep stronger skiers and boarders busy for days. There are many fairly easy descents, such as The Saddle, Last Chance, and Harmony Ridge. Harmony Bowl has a number of single black diamond runs such as McConkey's, Little Whistler, and Boomer Bowl, none of which are too terrifying. West Bowl is possibly the most testing, dominated by double black diamond runs: Cockalorium, Stefan's Chute, and Stefan's Salute. Those who merely want to take a peek at the bowls but are reluctant to try them can settle for easy options such as Burnt Stew Trail, Pika's Traverse, and Highway 86.

Whistler is also a useful location for embryonic heliskiers. Intrepid individuals can try it for a day before venturing into one of British Columbia's remote heliskiing lodges for a whole week of living side by side with fellow enthusiasts in a Bell 210 or an AStar helicopter. But with North America's highest vertical drop and some exceptional terrain here in Whistler, who needs a helicopter?

LAKE LOUISE & BANFF

ALBERTA, CANADA

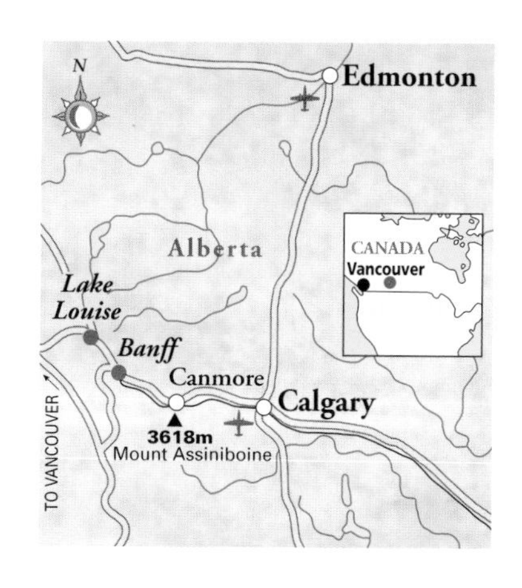

FAR FROM THE VAST INLAND SEAS OF PRAIRIE WHEAT, the great snow-capped peaks of the Canadian Rockies – the Alps of the new world – soar skyward. This epic scene of natural splendor brings skiers and snowboarders flocking to Alberta and British Columbia, but it was nature's bubbling forces below the ground that started the pilgrimage.

When Tom Wilson, a railroad surveyor, reportedly became the first white man to set eyes on what would become known as Lake Louise, he exclaimed in awe, "As God is my judge, I have never in all my explorations seen such a matchless scene." William Cornelius Van Horne, the vice president and general manager of the Canadian Pacific Railway (CPR) agreed, famously adding, "Since we can't export the scenery, we'll have to import the tourists."

As the great CPR drove a band of steel across the pristine wilderness and along the Bow River Valley in the fall of 1883, what would one day become the bustling town of Banff was still just "Siding 29." Close to what would be the border between Alberta and British Columbia, three railroad workers-cum-prospectors in need of a bath stumbled across some glorious natural hot springs on Sulphur Mountain. They plunged in, whooping with joy.

But any dreams of turning their discovery into profit were soon dashed – the land was government-owned. "These springs are worth a million dollars," said one state official. They were worth considerably more. The prime minister of the day, John Macdonald, quipped, "These springs will recuperate the patient and recoup the treasury."

TOP The scenery is there for everyone to see, regardless of their skiing or snowboarding ability. There are no major lifts at Louise that a novice cannot ride – every chair has an easy way down.

RIGHT A giant step for man in scenery that really beats the moon. Unlike many of their U.S. counterparts, Lake Louise's peaks are sharper and more alpine, and start from a lower altitude, which adds to their dramatic appearance.

In 1902 the boundaries were expanded to include Lake Louise, and in 1930 the area was declared the Banff National Park, encompassing 6641 square kilometers (2564 square miles) of mountains, lakes, rivers, canyons, and forests. Today it is one of Canada's finest and most scenic ski regions. Van Horne may have brought the tourists to the scenery, but even he could not take credit for bringing the wildlife to the tourists. One of the delights of Banff is that elk and long-horned sheep sometimes stroll around the streets, nibbling at the odd plant or even rummaging in trash cans.

The lake and the Canadian Rockies were indeed a matchless scene, and over the years the railroad brought tourists in the hundreds, and then thousands, to share the thrill of sightseeing in this staggeringly beautiful part of the world. Later, climbers, skiers, and snowboarders found their way here, too.

A century later, the spectacular peaks and the huge frozen lake, fed by six different glaciers that girdle the majestic Mount Victoria, still have the same mesmerizing effect on visitors. The visual impact of the awe-inspiring area named after Queen Victoria's fourth daughter – Louise Caroline Alberta – must rank as one of the finest in North America.

The Banff-Lake Louise ski area comprises an entire region and has three separate resorts – Mount Norquay, Sunshine Village, and Lake Louise itself – all very different and all rather spread out. Between them, they offer 223 runs served by 28 lifts – about 200km (130 miles) of skiing all told.

Mount Norquay, where Banff locals ski and board, was the first ski hill to be developed in the area, in 1926. Although the first rope tows did not arrive until 1942, Norquay installed Canada's first chair lift in 1948 – the very same year that Sunshine Village got its first rope tow, taking local skiers to areas that, until then, had been reached only by antiquated snowcats.

Today, Mount Norquay, although predominantly an intermediate resort, has some seriously steep expert trails, particularly off its North American double chair, which accesses only black diamond terrain like Memorial Bowl, Valley of the Ten, and Temptation.

In 1934 a cabin was built by CPR just below Sunshine Meadows, which skiers from Banff had been hiking up to for years. Within 10 years a lift had been added. The Sunshine ski area perched on the continental divide, with some of the highest slopes and most abundant snowfalls in Canada, had arrived. What it lacked were trees and shelter.

The addition of the considerably tree-clad Goat's Eye mountain – with runs inevitably playing on the goat connection: Billy Goat's Gruff, Scapegoat, and Goat's Head Soup – made Sunshine a major attraction.

LEFT The Fairmont Chateau Lake Louise is set in one of the world's most beautiful locations on the shores of the frozen lake named after Queen Victoria's fourth daughter.

LEFT Homegrown – when Lake Louise built its big new base lodge, transforming the lower mountain, the resort used pine trees cut from glades on the ski slopes.

The mountain, a spine-tingling mix of glade skiing and cruising runs, also invites visitors to try Goatchicken Glade and Goatsucker Glade.

With well over 100 designated trails and off-piste opportunities almost too extensive to mention, Lake Louise itself is by far the biggest player in the region. As you ride the Top of the World Express chair, the scenery is simply overwhelming. Following the Bow Valley, a vista of almost unsurpassed grandeur unfolds – mile after mile of craggy towering peaks, almost shoulder-to-shoulder, hanging blue glaciers, and green valley floors of thickly wooded spruce. The scenery is there for everyone to appreciate, regardless of their skiing or boarding ability, as there is virtually no major lift at Louise that a novice cannot ride. Every chair has an easy way down. On the front face, for example, beginners can take their time negotiating Wiwaxy while intermediates tackle Juniper. Meanwhile, the experts will be relishing the Men's Downhill. The Larch area has some easy runs, like Marmot and Lookout, interspersed with more challenging trails like Bobcat and Wolverine. Beyond this area are the Ptarmigan and Paradise Trails as well as the Back Bowls – a veritable "jewelry box" of ski-able backcountry.

There is some exhilarating off-piste from the Ptarmigan Chair, including double black diamond runs like Exhibition Trees and Ptarmigan Chutes. The Summit Platter takes skiers up and over the shoulder of Mount Whitehorn (2672m; 8765ft) to access Chunky's, North Cornice, and Shoulder Roll – or easy blue "escape lanes" like Skyline or Boomerang. The Paradise Chair takes skiers high onto a ridge where they are spoiled for choice. They can either make for a variety of black and double black diamond runs in Louise's "Diamond Mine" – Paradise Cornice, Paradise Bowl, and Soul Bowl – or take the easy way down via the green Saddleback trail. West Bowl offers sensational views down to the lake where the Chateau, like a matchbox-sized fairy-tale castle, hovers on the waterfront surrounded by a deep green forest. Sadly, Queen Victoria never witnessed it.

RESORT	LAKE LOUISE & BANFF
GETTING THERE:	Calgary: 185km (115 miles); Banff: 60km (35 miles). Daily train and bus services from Banff and Calgary. Free and frequent shuttle services to ski area offered by some hotels in Lake Louise.
HEIGHT:	1645–2640m (5400–8660ft)
NO. OF LIFTS:	11
TYPES OF PISTES:	25% beg, 45% inter, 30% adv.
MAIN ADVANTAGES:	Tree skiing; stunning scenery; easy runs from top of mountain.
DRAWBACKS:	Long drive from Banff town; lift lines on peak holidays.

FERNIE

BRITISH COLUMBIA, CANADA

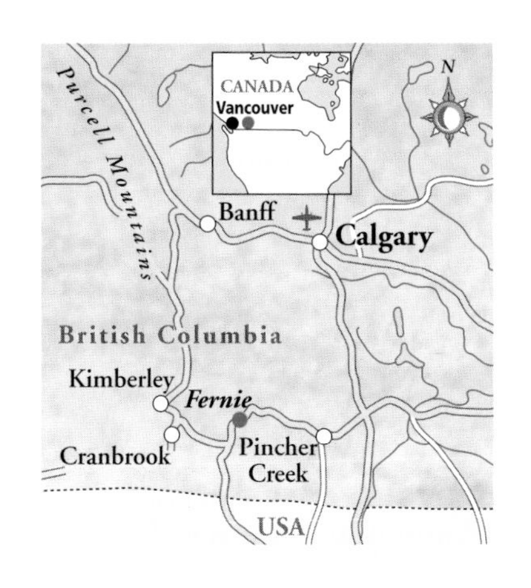

FROM THE AUTHOR'S LOG, 15TH OF MARCH 1998: "In our spectacular journey to a new star of the British Columbian firmament of ski areas, we have boldly gone down a ski trail called Deep Space and discovered that while the natives are definitely friendly, the terrain here is as challenging as anything in the Canadian Rockies. Falling Star might have been an easier option, but the snow is so deep it almost doesn't matter."

If "steep and deep" is your goal, seek no further than Fernie, a ski area on the southeastern tip of British Columbia that, until fairly recently, was little known outside Canada. It is rare these days to catch a newcomer just before it blossoms into a major player, but a few years ago some of us were lucky enough to visit Fernie before the transition that set it on the road to fame and, who knows, possibly fortune.

The town of Fernie was founded just over a century ago when an extraordinary English adventurer, William Fernie, drifted into this part of British Columbia after wandering the globe. Returning from Australia via Peru and California, he encountered an Indian chieftain's daughter wearing a necklace of shining black stones, which he recognized as coal. Promising to marry her if the chief agreed to show him where the coal had been found, Fernie later reneged on the deal, and the chieftain swore that the town would suffer fire, flood, and famine. It all came true. Finally, in August 1964, Chief Red Eagle of the Kootenay tribes ceremonially lifted the Fernie curse by smoking a peace pipe with the mayor.

TOP Parents wanting to enjoy the advanced slopes on their own can leave children in the capable hands of ski instructors at the daycare center in Fernie.

RIGHT Fernie's generous snow record was once known only to the cognoscenti, but even though the secret is out now, the slopes can still be uncrowded.

The somewhat run-down old mining town is full of character and deliciously ungentrified, but one can already see how easily it could develop into a Canadian Telluride or even another Aspen. Charlie Locke, at the time the biggest individual player in Canadian skiing, took steps toward this development when he purchased Fernie a few years ago, adding to a portfolio that already included Lake Louise and several Canadian resorts in both the Rockies and Quebec.

Almost immediately, Locke doubled the size of Fernie's remarkable terrain by building new lifts in magnificent bowl areas formerly almost entirely the preserve of snowcat skiers. As a result, the Timber Bowl high-speed quad was able to take skiers and snowboarders into picturesque intermediate terrain in the heart of Siberia Bowl and Timber Bowl, while the White Pass quad opened up more inviting trails in Currie Bowl. One run, Falling Star, provides a wonderful treat for novice skiers and boarders, right down Siberia Bowl, a beautiful area that was previously inaccessible. Currie Powder does much the same thing from the top of Currie Bowl.

Fernie has always been cherished for the steep, daunting-looking front-face trails high above the base area, which can intimidate new arrivals. The big three certainly live up to their names: Stag Leap, Sky Dive, and Decline. Yet, as so often happens with runs that seem impossibly steep, when inspected from closer quarters at the top, they seem reassuringly less dramatic.

The terrain, which appeals as much as any to those in pursuit of the steep and the deep, is reached by taking the recently installed Great Bear Express quad chair and then accessing the somewhat tricky Face Lift rope tow (a.k.a. the Lift From Hell), which brings you to Lizard Bowl. From here the big decision is whether to turn left or right.

Skier's left brings you down Cruiser, a scenic blue run, to the top of the Boomerang Chair and beyond. From here there are all kinds of exhilarating "shots" through the trees: Boomerang, for example, and

ABOVE The new Cornerstone Lodge is just one of many new slopeside apartments and hotels designed to give an international flavor to the area now known as Fernie Alpine Resort.

Linda's Run. Boomerang Ridge is an even steeper double-black run. Skier's right takes you toward what I would call the real meat of the mountain, a steep ridge with some exceptionally good glades, including Concussion, Tom's Run, Cornice Chute, and Barracuda. Some, like Windows and Sunnyside 44 – so called because of its unusually steep pitch of 44 degrees – are not even on the trail map.

Many of Fernie's slopes are like Sunnyside 44 – just a little steeper than you might be comfortable with. Hard-core skiers and boarders will love it. Of course the Face Lift does access easier runs, too. There is an assortment of blue runs and Cascade, Bow, Weasel, Bear, and Cruiser are easier alternatives to the derring-do variety. As for steep runs, Deep Space is still out there, but somewhat to my chagrin it has been officially added to the trail map. No longer is it the captain's little secret.

ABOVE Having conquered Elk – a gentle beginner slope – a Fernie Mountain Host suggests an intermediate run down Lower Bear before tackling some of the resort's sterner stuff.

RESORT	FERNIE
GETTING THERE:	Calgary: 300km (185 miles); Cranbrook: 100km (60 miles); Fernie town: 4km (2½ miles). Bus and taxi services available from Calgary and Cranbrook. Frequent daily shuttle services from downtown Fernie to the resort.
HEIGHT:	1070–1920m (3510–6300ft)
NO OF LIFTS:	9
TYPES OF PISTES:	30% beginner, 40% intermediate, 30% advanced.
MAIN ADVANTAGES:	Extensive range of skiing; excellent snow record.
DRAWBACKS:	Limited après-ski; small downtown area, limited selection of mountain restaurants.

ASPEN

COLORADO

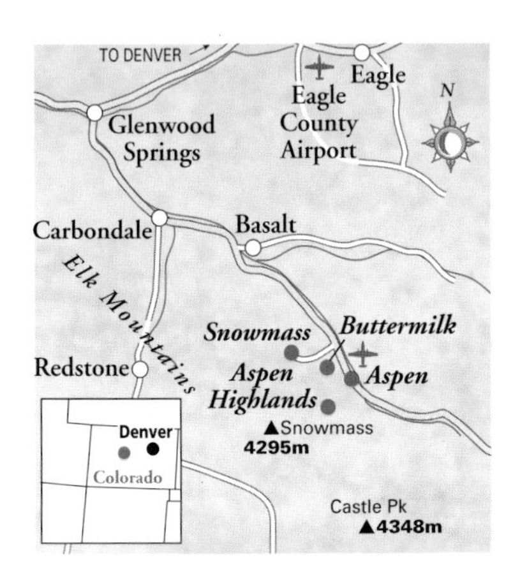

IF YOU ARE LOOKING FOR HOLLYWOOD ON ICE, and you scratch the surface hard enough, you will eventually find a rich vein in Aspen. On the other hand, this friendly Colorado ski town can be surprisingly unpretentious.

Aspen likes to boast, "There's only one." Should this claim make you a trifle anxious – perhaps you have heard tales of glitz and glamour – go straight to the J Bar at the oldest hotel in town, the Jerome, and order a drink. You will instantly feel at home. This is, after all – in the days when Aspen was a ramshackle collection of old buildings called Ute City – where miners used to celebrate a precious strike of silver. There was nothing precious about the town, however, and despite the hype this is still largely true today.

When people talk about skiing in Aspen, they are generally referring to Ajax Mountain, which rises directly above the town. However, there are actually four ski mountains linked to the name of Aspen, all available on the same lift ticket. Moving down the Roaring Fork Valley, the next resort is Aspen Highlands (technically the most challenging), followed by Buttermilk, frequently acclaimed as the best beginner mountain in the Rockies, and finally Snowmass, an area bigger than the other three combined, which prides itself on its extensive intermediate terrain (but has plenty of extreme slopes, too).

Even though Aspen Highlands has now acquired a completely new base village, there is no substitute for the old town. Some of the buildings are now genuinely quite old (at least in U.S. terms) with décor hinting at everything from Art Nouveau to Art Deco. Victorian streetlights and fairy lights twinkle all winter along the cobblestone sidewalks and pedestrian malls.

TOP They don't call it Aspen for nothing – an elegant archway of these Aspen poplars adds charm to the slopes at America's most famous resort.

RIGHT There's "only one" Aspen – but four mountains. Snowmass, by far the biggest, is celebrated for a series of parallel intermediate runs that effectively form a trail almost a mile wide.

Among the intriguing legacies from the old mining days on Ajax mountain are the so-called "dump" runs with names like Bear Paw, Zaugg Dump, Perry's Prowl, Last Dollar, and Short Snort; all fairly short, sharp, and challenging descents built on the steep slopes where miners once tunneled their way into the mountain. There are still two working silver mines today – one, the Compromise mine, is hidden away on the slopes directly above the town, just to one side of two double black diamond runs, Silver Queen and Silver Rush.

Beginners are discouraged from skiing Ajax, not so much because the terrain is particularly difficult, but because getting off the mountain at the end of the day can be seriously intimidating. Most of the easier skiing is at the top of the mountain but the main exit slopes, Copper Bowl and Spar Gulch, tend to be somewhat fast and furious thoroughfares down which intermediates and experts plunge on their way home. Unless beginners "download" (travel back down) on the Silver Queen gondola, they are forced into the very same narrow, rather steep gullies to take their chances with the Exocet-like maneuvers of their more confident peers. They would fare better at Buttermilk. Largely a beginner mountain, it should certainly not be sneered at; intermediates will find plenty to keep them amused for a day or so, and after powder days even strong skiers can be found there.

Aspen Highlands is Aspen's real secret weapon. Highlands, now cozily ensconced in the Aspen's happy family of resorts, was once a huge thorn in its side. The only one of the four to be independently owned, it had developed a gung-ho reputation for the most challenging but cheapest skiing in the Roaring Fork Valley. While the more sedate celebrity residents and tourists would scarcely ski anywhere but Ajax, hard-core skiers would head straight for the antiquated lift system and deliciously steep slopes of Highlands' Olympic Bowl, Steeple Chase and what is now Temerity, skiing exhilarating runs like Mushroom, Aces & Eights and Deception, which starts steep and gets steeper. Highlands became a cult area – a tailor-made haunt for impecunious, self-styled ski bums, and an opportunity for them to thumb their noses at the well-groomed skiers cruising the slopes on Ajax.

When Aspen acquired Highlands, it set about upgrading the lifts, facilitating the birth of a completely new ski village. Almost overnight, Aspen Highlands became something to be raved instead of ranted about. The skiing, of course, has not changed; in fact it has improved. The less challenging slopes are better-groomed, the lifts are faster, and the resort has opened up even more challenging off-piste terrain in the so-called Y-zones, B-Zones, and the recently opened G-Zones in Highland Bowl.

Although Snowmass is the furthest resort from the town of Aspen, it should really not be missed. It may not be as fashionable as Ajax, but it has a wonderful variety of excellent intermediate terrain, as well as plenty of skiing for novices and experts. The Big Burn is Snowmass's signature slope. Several trails run parallel through the Burn area, giving skiers and boarders what is effectively a single trail almost a mile wide in which to wander to their hearts content, dipping in and out of the trees when the fancy takes them. As for Aspen itself, you have to take the old silver mining town as you find it. But do take it – there is indeed "only one."

RESORT	ASPEN
GETTING THERE:	Denver: 355km (220 miles); Eagle County airport: 110km (70 miles). Aspen has own airport, 5km (3 miles) from resort.
HEIGHT:	Snowmass: 2400–3800m (7870–12,470ft) Ajax: 2420–3400m (7940–11,160ft)
NO. OF LIFTS:	39
TYPES OF PISTES:	Snowmass: 7% beg, 55% inter, 38% adv. Ajax: 35% inter, 65% adv.
MAIN ADVANTAGES:	Large area with four mountains to choose from; lively towns with good selection of shops and restaurants.
DRAWBACKS:	Snowmass, the biggest area, is a 20km (12-mile) trip.

ABOVE LEFT Although Aspen tries to downplay its glitzy image, it's easy to shop till you drop in the pedestrian malls, where most of the better-known designer stores can be found.

OPPOSITE Aspen has many Victorian houses such as these on East Hopkins Avenue, remnants of the Gold Rush days in the late 1800s.

JACKSON HOLE

WYOMING

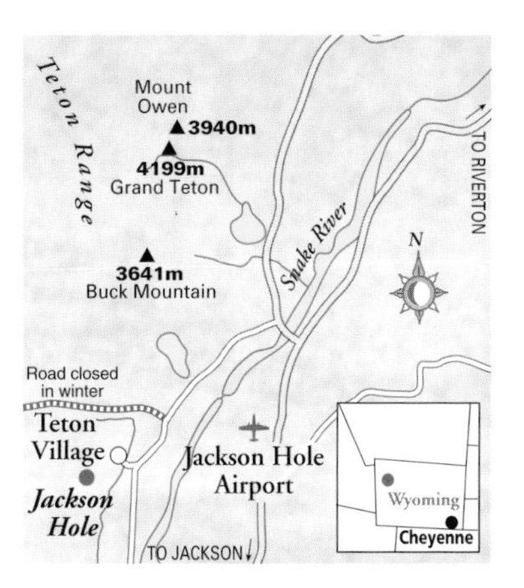

ON A CLEAR DAY, THE TOY-TOWN AIRPORT OF Jackson Hole, Wyoming, offers an unforgettable ringside view of a frozen tidal wave of granite: the fabulous Tetons. When the sun glints on these mountains as they rear up from the valley floor, or "hole," the extraordinary grandeur of the Cathedral Group comprising the Grand, Upper, and Middle Tetons, plus Mounts Owen, Teewinot, and Nez Perce Peak, is mesmerizing. Many of these soaring peaks have been skied, but only by a handful of extreme skiers.

When Jackson Hole's founder, Paul McCollister, went searching for a new ski area in this spectacular range, he settled on a wonderful mountain called Rendezvous a little to the south of the Cathedral Group, built a base community at Teton Village, and installed a bright red Tram (cable car) to take skiers to the top.

It may not be the Grand Teton, but nobody has anything but respect for Rendezvous Mountain. How could you not, when a sign at the top of the Tram informs you, "Our mountain is like nothing you have skied before. It is huge, with variable terrain, from groomed slopes to dangerous cliff areas and dangerously variable weather and snow conditions. You must always exercise extreme caution. You could make a mistake and suffer personal injury or death. Give this mountain the respect it deserves."

A mellower neighboring mountain, Après Vous, enables beginners and intermediates who might find the Rendezvous slopes daunting, to enjoy exciting but uncomplicated cruising on trails like Werner and Moran. The Bridger Gondola between the two mountains provides intermediate terrain and takes the pressure off the Tram, which is the key to Jackson's best in-bounds skiing.

LEFT Once seen, never forgotten – the awe-inspiring jagged peaks of Jackson Hole's Cathedral Group. The Grand, Upper, and Middle Tetons stand shoulder to shoulder with Mount Owen, Mount Teewinot, and Nez Perce Peak.

TOP The strategically placed Bridger Gondola takes the pressure off Jackson Hole's flagship Tram cable car and accesses good intermediate terrain between the gung-ho slopes of Rendezvous Mountain and the easy-does-it cruising on Après Vous.

The top of Rendezvous can be a ferocious place in stern weather. Furthermore, there is no really easy way down. Even by traversing the East Ridge, sooner or later skiers and boarders are forced down Rendezvous Bowl. This is not the most difficult descent in the world, but it is certainly challenging – particularly if snow conditions are tricky – and can be beyond the lower intermediate's ability. This is unfortunate, because once skiers and snowboarders have negotiated this initial minefield the mountain opens up to all kinds of attractions.

Rendezvous Trail is one of the most exhilarating sections of the mountain. A real roller coaster, it also offers all kinds of options for bailing out into interesting terrain on the way down. If you can resist leaping into Central Chute or Bivouac, you will find something even more tempting in the Hobacks. This is Jackson's most famous "in-bounds" back-country ski area – a long valley with skiing off both ridges and opportunities to make endless turns in deep snow until exhaustion stops you in your tracks.

The most famous challenge on Rendezvous is Corbet's Couloir, a yawning chasm near the top of the mountain within full view of the Tram. Skiers and boarders must leap at least 3m (10ft) before they land, and are forced to turn almost immediately to avoid a rock face. The alternative route involves a jump closer to 6m (20ft), but at least this means you can keep going all the way down without worrying too much about rocks.

There is an abundance of chutes, gullies, and cirques all over the mountain. Alta, Expert, and Tower Three chutes – steep, "double-fall line," gladed runs – provide less extreme challenges. Others include Paint Brush, Toilet Bowl, and the Headwall, a wonderful descent in deep snow.

ABOVE Teton Village, at Jackson Hole in Wyoming, exudes a lively frontier feel and is reminiscent of Wild West days, when cowboys tethered their horses outside the saloons.

Hiking to nearby Cody Peak accesses "runs" that make some of Jackson's tougher in-bounds trails look routine. Some are genuinely extreme. Until quite recently, Cody was the haunt of the ski patrol and hard-core locals, who were only allowed access to it as spring approached. Then Jackson decided to open the gates to the skiing public, who can now enjoy 1100 hectares (2500 acres) of its legendary back-country skiing terrain in the Bridger-Teton National Forest throughout winter. At the same time, the resort set up a full-scale Alpine-style guiding service for off-piste adventures.

Rock Springs and Green River Canyons – with steep pitches like Space Walk and Zero G – are two rather more mellow valleys below Cody Peak that run parallel with the Hobacks. You might even persuade an off-duty ski patroller to introduce you to the likes of Endless Couloir, Air Force Couloir, Mile Long Couloir, and Cardiac Ridge on the opposite side of the ski area in Grand Teton National Park where the guide service does not operate. Do try also to make the scenic drive over the Teton Pass to the other side of the Tetons to ski in Grand Targhee, which has some of the best powder skiing in the Rockies. The town of Jackson also has its own ski area at Snow King.

Another great attraction at Jackson is the chance of seeing some fascinating wildlife. Moose, elk, coyotes, and eagles are not uncommon, and it is well worth taking a day off from the slopes to visit what is probably the world's biggest elk sanctuary. Make sure you visit the town of Jackson, a lively old Wild West town with several good restaurants and designer stores. Step inside the Million Dollar Cowboy Bar, if only to soak up the atmosphere: pool tables, live bands, and dude cowboys swigging beers and margaritas, sitting on leather saddles perched on the bar stools. This really is skiing the Wild West.

RESORT	JACKSON HOLE
GETTING THERE:	Idaho Falls airport: 140km (85 miles), daily shuttle service available; Targhee to Jackson: 75km (45 miles); Jackson Hole airport: 13km (8 miles).
HEIGHT:	Jackson: 1920–3190m (6300–10,470ft) Targhee: 2440–3100m (8000–10,170ft)
NO. OF LIFTS:	Jackson: 11; Targhee: 4
TYPES OF PISTES:	Jackson: 10% beg, 40% inter, 50% adv. Targhee: 10% beg, 70% inter, 20% adv.
MAIN ADVANTAGES:	Snow-sure resort; large ski area; cowboy-style après-ski; superb scenery; close to Yellowstone National Park.
DRAWBACKS:	Jackson town separate from ski area at Teton Village; remote location.

LAKE TAHOE

CALIFORNIA/NEVADA

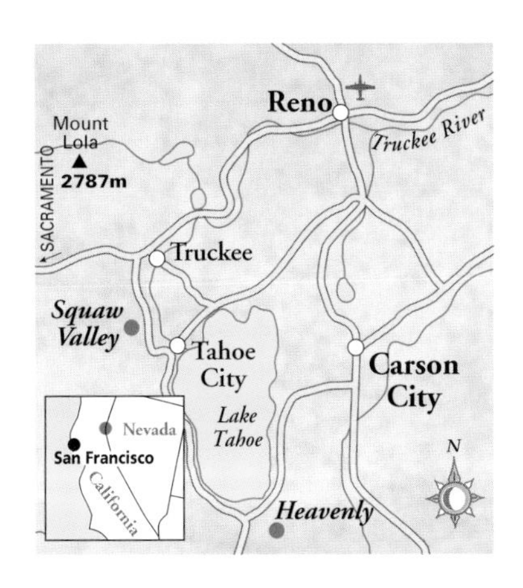

IN 1853 THE *PLACERVILLE HERALD* REPORTED from the Tahoe Basin, "Gold has been found along the base of the Carson-Sierra Range. It is a magnificent lake. It will become a world-renowned place." The newspaper was right about everything except the gold. Mark Twain agreed. Lake Tahoe was, he wrote, "a noble sheet of blue water, lifted 6300ft (1900m) above the level of the sea, and walled in by a rim of snow-clad mountain peaks – brilliantly photographed upon its still surface." When Les Otten's American Skiing Company purchased Heavenly ski area, he described it rather more prosaically: "We have casinos like Monte Carlo, mountains like the Alps, a magnificent lake and 24-hour nightlife."

Treating this gorgeous cobalt-blue high-alpine lake, surrounded by 15 ski areas, as one giant ski arena is cheating slightly, but since the ski areas themselves refer to Lake Tahoe as a resort, it is tempting not to have to single out just one of them. The lake, split roughly into two-thirds California, one-third Nevada, is indeed breathtaking. So much so that it almost doesn't matter which resort you choose to ski in. Some, like Diamond Peak have more sensational views, but are not necessarily the biggest or best ski areas. Others, like Squaw Valley, have superb skiing but are too far away to have significant lake views. Be adventurous! Why not base yourself in one location, rent a car, and visit a handful?

The word Tahoe is an Indian name meaning "water in a high place." Lake Tahoe, one of the world's biggest and highest alpine lakes is almost entirely surrounded by mountains. Between them, the 15 ski areas have a grand total of 27,000 acres (12,000 hectares) of ski terrain, 200 lifts,

TOP Few resorts in the world offer such beautiful "air" as Heavenly, a ski area that almost lives up to its name: all this and 14 more ski areas around the shimmering cobalt-blue waters of Lake Tahoe.

RIGHT In a good powder year, exhilarating tree skiing dramatically increases Heavenly's terrain. And if the snow just happens to be a little late, the resort claims the biggest snow-making system in the West.

and more than 1000 trails. Heavenly, with the highest slopes at over 3000m (10,000ft), is the destination resort most people link with Lake Tahoe, with Squaw Valley a close second. Although Heavenly – spread like the lake across the California-Nevada border – is high, it takes no chances with snow cover and claims the largest snow-making system on the West Coast.

It is also involved in a 10-year, multimillion-dollar redevelopment plan, including new hotels, villages, lifts, and a new base area – combined with a full-scale "makeover" for the lakeside Stateline resort community that straddles the border near the Californian base. From here, an eight-person gondola now feeds a new six-passenger high-speed chair climbing from mid-mountain on the California side to near the top of the Nevada side.

Heavenly, with more than 85 trails, is famous for exhilarating cruising and glorious lake views. From the top of Monument Peak, as you traverse into Nevada, the view becomes even more extraordinary: Lake Tahoe on one side, and the Carson Valley desert on the other. In good powder years, the extensive gladed areas dramatically increase the skiable acreage. The white-barked Western pines, a rare species of stunted fir, make for wonderful tree skiing.

For real off-piste challenges, skiers and boarders should head for Killebrew Canyon and Mott Canyon, where double black diamond chutes and bowls offer excellent powder skiing. Mogul lovers will want to test their legs on Gunbarrel. Some skiers, who call themselves the Face Rats, do almost nothing else but ski this seemingly endless bump run, managing as many as 40 descents in one day. Recently two Rats pushed the record up to 54, but most people settle for one.

Heavenly is also famous for its huge Las Vegas-style gambling hotels. There are glittering shows at places like Harrah's, Harvey's, and Caesar's in South Lake Tahoe, and a visit can be quite intriguing, even if it is only to watch the hopeful tugging at hundreds of fruit machines in the vast gambling areas, often persevering until dawn.

Legend has it that Squaw Valley was discovered as long ago as 500 A.D. by the Washoe Indians. In the 1860s rumors of rich silver deposits brought prospectors flocking to the valley, but nothing was found. The area did, however, finally hit pay dirt when it was selected for the 1960 Winter Games. Squaw is fortunate in having six impressive granite mountains for skiers and boarders to choose from. In spite of Squaw Peak's celebrated Palisades chutes, which feature in any number of extreme skiing videos, much of the remaining terrain offers equally enjoyable easy skiing.

Broken Arrow is a good mix, while Snow King, Granite Chief, and K22 – so called because the original owner's wife had to make 22 kick turns to get down it – are more challenging. Unusually, the resort's main nursery slopes are on top of a mountain – Emigrant Peak – rather than at the base. This gives beginners the wonderful opportunity of an exceptionally long run all the way down to the base area at the end of the day – one of the most thrilling beginner runs in the entire United States.

Like Heavenly, Squaw is vast, with 1800 hectares (4000 acres) of virtually "ski where you like" terrain. There are no named trails as such, just an endless array of big, wide-open bowls, bump runs, and chutes, described by a colleague as "a hundred different chutes, cliffs, steep bumps, and hairball rock bands – most of them open to the public."

Squaw's neighbor, Alpine Meadows, is almost a replica of Squaw on a smaller scale, but with equal challenges. Northstar-at-Tahoe has no fewer than seven terrain parks and outstanding views of the lake. But of all the major Tahoe resorts, Kirkwood – more remote than many – is probably the least known outside California. Its new mountain village, accommodating 2000 additional skiers, will no doubt bring it to the attention of a wider international market. Both the skiing and the landscape – a huge amphitheater of rugged ridges and craggy peaks – are superb. Exhilarating "steeps and deeps" like The Wall, Sentinel Bowl, and Palisades Bowl, provide hard-core skiers with magnificent terrain. The last word on this stunning lake area should go, perhaps, to the ever-eloquent Mark Twain who said, "To obtain the air the angels breathe, you must go to Tahoe."

RESORT	LAKE TAHOE
GETTING THERE:	Reno to Heavenly: 180km (110 miles); Reno to Squaw Valley: 60km (35 miles); Squaw: 8km (5 miles) north of Lake Tahoe and Tahoe City. Heavenly is in the heart of South Lake Tahoe, good base for visiting other resorts.
HEIGHT:	Heavenly: 2000–3000m (6560–10,000ft) Squaw: 1900–2650m (6230–8690ft)
NO. OF LIFTS:	Heavenly: 29; Squaw: 30
TYPES OF PISTES:	Heavenly: 20% beg, 45% inter, 35% adv. Squaw: 25% beg, 45% inter, 30% adv.
MAIN ADVANTAGES:	Large selection of ski resorts around lake; lots of tree skiing available; outstanding scenery.
DRAWBACKS:	Car necessary if wanting to access all areas; limited traditional "alpine charm."

OPPOSITE Over 20km (12 miles) wide and 35km (20 miles) long, Tahoe is one of the world's largest and highest alpine lakes. You can even take your skis from one shore to another by paddle steamer, enjoying an après-ski party on the return trip.

VAIL

COLORADO

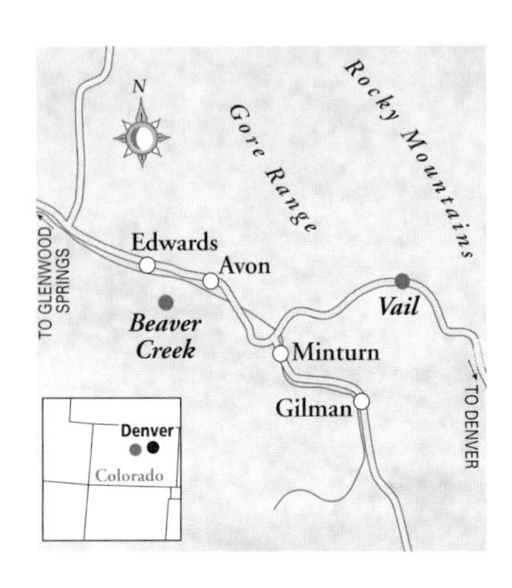

ONE DAY IT WAS A SHEEP MOUNTAIN. THE NEXT, says one guide book, it was an "internationally famous ski resort." Unlike Aspen, Telluride, and Breckenridge, Vail's history dates back merely to the early 1960s, when Earl Eaton stumbled across what was to become Vail Mountain while prospecting for uranium in Eagle County.

You could not really see it from the road, so Eaton dragged his friend Pete Seibert up to have a closer look. Easier said than done. The two men strapped on skis and, after climbing through deep snow for seven hours, finally crested the summit. "The first time I saw it," said Seibert, "I knew it was as good as any ski mountain I'd seen." Beyond the valley rose the pinnacles of the Gore Range, named after one of Colorado's most bizarre tourists.

An Irish baronet known as Lord Gore, famously led perhaps the most extravagantly equipped and most shameful hunting party ever seen in the Rockies. Gore and his crew, along with 100 horses, 40 oxen, and 50 hunting hounds, arrived in Colorado in 1854. According to a local author, June Simonton, his impedimenta included a green and white silk tent with carpeted floor, a bathtub, brass bedstead, and even "a commode with a fur-lined seat." To help trade with local Indians, Gore also brought 250 gallons of 180-proof grain-alcohol that, flavored with red pepper and plug tobacco, turned into a poisonous brew known as trade whisky. It was said that, "You could drink trade whisky, and you could get shot and killed, but you wouldn't die till you sobered up."

TOP The ultimate in Colorado glitz, Vail's sister resort of Beaver Creek – the "smartest address" in the valley – was finally completed at the turn of the 20th century. Now, without the building sites, the wealthy residents can enjoy some peace and tranquility.

RIGHT Although Vail dislikes comparisons with Aspen, its big rival, it cannot deny that these graceful aspens provide magical tree skiing. America's biggest single mountain has 175 marked trails, but there's still plenty of room for off-piste.

Gore and his friends proceeded to chase and shoot every deer, elk, antelope, and buffalo within range, taking only the biggest as trophies and leaving the rest to rot. The Uncpapa Sioux were so indignant at the depletion of their food supply that they finally surrounded Gore and his men, "stripped them of their horses and supplies and every last stitch of clothing, and suggested they leave the country." This, after wandering naked in the wilderness, grubbing for roots and berries, they finally did.

Fast forward a century or so. Around 1960, when the pedestrianized village was still in the construction stage, a local rancher put up a sign saying, "Stay Out! Anyone Coming In Here Will Be Shot To Hell!" Today it is your knees that get shot to hell with so much skiing. Vail claims to be the single biggest ski mountain in the United States. And it probably is.

It hardly seems possible that the resort, once the parvenu of Colorado skiing and unkindly dubbed a "plastic Bavaria" because of its Austrian pretensions, is 40 years old. Still in many ways the new kid on the block, Vail is also one of the most powerful. Too powerful, perhaps, and too corporate – there is a sense that when you come to Vail, and increasingly its sister resorts of Beaver Creek, Breckenridge, and Keystone, you are the guest of a major conglomerate increasingly driven by a corporate mentality.

Big, beautifully groomed, but a little bland, Vail has wonderful cruising on runs like Lodgepole, Ledges, and Born Free and serious bumps on Blue Ox or Roger's Run. And, apart from being big, Vail has one more unique selling point: its legendary "back bowls," augmented as a special millennium treat for both aspiring and seasoned back-country skiers, by the opening of Blue Sky Basin.

The back bowls – huge bowl-shaped areas where the snow is left to nature's whim – are a seemingly endless 1200-hectare (2700-acre) system incorporating Game Creek, Sun Up, Sun Down, Tea Cup, China, Siberia, and Mongolia bowls. Evocative trail names include Rasputin's Revenge and Genghis Khan. For an exceptional run, find a local to show you the way from Game Creek to the Minturn Mile. This starts with a steep and exhilarating gladed bowl running into a remote river valley where the skiing becomes a little awkward (along narrow paths following the stream). Eventually, after rather more than a mile, you reach the small town of Minturn. A drink in the Saloon – once a favorite with John Wayne and occasionally visited by Clint Eastwood – is a must. But unless you have laid on your own transport, you will need to take a bus or taxi back to Vail.

Vail's original sister resort, the even more upmarket Beaver Creek, just 14km (9 miles) down the road, also has excellent cruising but its claim to fame are the Birds of Prey runs like Bald Eagle, Osprey, and Falcon Park on Grouse Mountain. Screech Owl is a particular favorite of mine – hauntingly beautiful and superb in fresh powder. During what has become an early destination for the World Cup season, the classic Golden Eagle trail becomes the Birds of Prey Men's Downhill Course.

But it is Vail and Beaver Creek's intermediate terrain that attracts the bulk of their visitors. There are blue runs simply everywhere – more than 100 spread between the two resorts. A whole network starts from Eagle's Nest Ridge; Pickeroon, Berries, Lodgepole, and Ledges are all good. Lodgepole, with its roller coaster descent is another favorite, and Born Free, which starts just alongside Adventure Ridge at Eagle's Nest, is a must. At night, Adventure Ridge becomes a floodlit after-hours recreational park with a dance club and restaurants where diners can watch night skiing, boarding, tubing, and ice skating. There is also a children's snowmobile track (adults can enjoy snowmobile tours at twilight, sunsets included), a children's sledding park, and ski-bike tours.

On Beaver Creek's Centennial, with green, blue, and black sections, skiers will find a magnificent top-to-bottom ride all the way from the start of the Men's Downhill at 3490m (11,440ft) to the base area, a vertical drop of over 1000m (3300ft). A word of warning: Centennial gives you a rush. Try to avoid skiing Golden Eagle immediately afterward, or you might find yourself soaring a little too high for comfort.

LEFT Airforce One! Those who claim that Vail's skiing can sometimes be a little bland have obviously never tried this. This skier has luckily left a little snow for the next high flier. Challenges like this are not easy to find in Vail and the locals like to keep them to themselves.

RESORT	VAIL
GETTING THERE:	Denver to Beaver Creek: 220km (135 miles); Denver to Vail: 200km (120 miles); Beaver Creek only 40km (25 miles) from Eagle County airport. Shuttle from Denver and Eagle County airports. Train services from Denver.
HEIGHT:	Vail: 2470–3550m (8100–11,650ft) Beaver Creek: 2250–3500m (7380–11,480ft)
NO. OF LIFTS:	Vail: 33; Beaver Creek: 14
TYPES OF PISTES:	Vail: 18% beg, 29% inter, 53% adv. Beaver Creek: 34% beg, 39% inter, 27% adv.
MAIN ADVANTAGES:	Well-groomed slopes; plenty of tree skiing; friendly customer service-oriented resorts.
DRAWBACKS:	Few thrills for hard-core skiers; can be expensive.

PARK CITY, SNOWBIRD & ALTA

UTAH

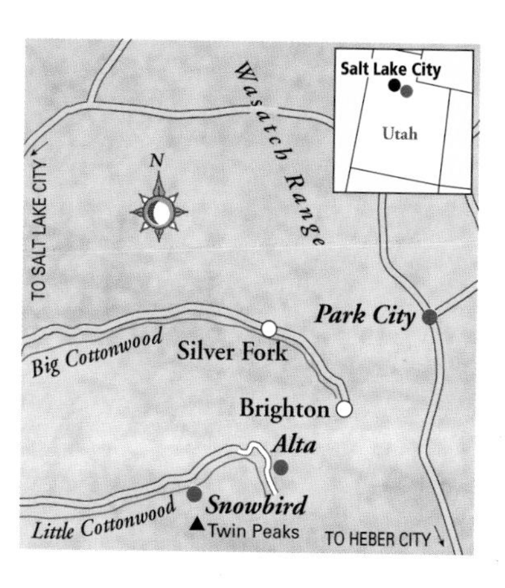

SALT LAKE CITY IS THE GATEWAY TO A RICHLY diverse network of nearby ski areas. Alta, just one hour or so from the airport, was once the essence of high adventure, living out the Hollywood version of an out-of-control, lawless society in which life was cheap and riotous behavior was on tap. Alta had one of the highest murder rates in the West, with countless brawls and shoot-outs taking place at bars with such evocative names as the Bucket of Blood Saloon. In between shooting each other, however, the miners did something constructive – they learned to ski. Little did they know that while their town would disappear (destroyed by an avalanche in the 1920s), a space-age resort called Snowbird would spring up in their backyard in the late 1960s, beneath the spectacular landmark of Utah's Twin Peaks.

Not far away, a much bigger mining community had spawned another of America's most important ski towns. Park City was once a wonderful mixture of precariously perched homes, false-fronted shops, smoky saloons, theaters, churches, brothels, and a Chinatown. Even today, its characterful main street reflects those days when it was the site of the largest silver-mining camp in the country.

When Park City Mountain Resort opened in 1963 it was known as Treasure Mountain. Skiers were transported nearly 5km (3 miles) into the mountain on the Spiro Tunnel mine train and then lifted vertically 550m (1800ft) to the slopes on a mine hoist elevator. Aerial trams once used for hauling ore were converted into chair lifts. There are still well over 1600km (1000 miles) of old silver-mine tunnels beneath the slopes, and old mining buildings and relics can still be seen by the side of some trails.

LEFT Where the silver-mine moguls once ruled, moguls made by skiers now cover the mountain. There are upwards of 1600km (1000 miles) of old mining tunnels beneath bump runs like this at Park City.

TOP Cardinal rule when you're skiing Utah's "Greatest Snow on Earth": Keep your mouth shut. On the other hand, if like Shad Snell you can't resist whooping for joy, expect to breathe a few snow crystals into your lungs.

Park City, one of the few Utah towns established by non-mormons, is a community with an enviable portfolio of ski areas. Deer Valley has developed a reputation as one of America's most pampering ski resorts.

RESORT	PARK CITY, SNOWBIRD & ALTA
GETTING THERE:	Salt Lake City airport to Park City: 60km (35 miles); Salt Lake City airport to Alta: 40km (25 miles); Salt Lake City airport to Snowbird: 50km (30 miles). Train and bus services from Salt Lake City.
HEIGHT:	Park City: 2100–3000m (6900–10,000ft) Alta: 2600–3215m (8530–10,550ft) Snowbird: 2470–3350m (8100–11,000ft)
NO OF LIFTS:	Park City: 15; Alta:13; Snowbird: 12
TYPES OF PISTES:	Park City: 18% beg, 44% inter, 38% adv. Alta: 25% beg, 40% inter, 35% adv. Snowbird: 25% beg, 35% inter, 40% adv.
MAIN ADVANTAGES:	Lots of ski areas near Salt Lake City; good snow record; spa at Snowbird; excellent resort base at Park City.
DRAWBACKS:	Limited après-ski in some resorts; 4WD vehicle needed to ensure access to all areas.

Attendants help unload your skis before you tackle some of the most meticulously groomed slopes in the country. There was once a joke that no matter how elderly or infirm the skier, the runs were so smooth it was almost impossible to fall over. Following remarks that it had "lots of diamonds but not enough black ones," the resort changed its image by opening up tougher skiing areas. There is even a trail map for experts.

Park City Mountain Resort is more in keeping with the town's colorful past. One light-hearted explanation of why it has never merged with its neighbor is that the rather refined skiers at genteel Deer Valley might not wish to rub shoulders with Park City Mountain Resort's more down-to-earth visitors – and vice versa.

Many of the trails at Park City have names that echo the old mining days; Silver Cliff, The Hoist, Prospector, Bonanza, and Shaft are just a few. Challenging runs like Silver King, Erika's Gold, and Crescent tumble down from Claim Jumper toward the resort center. Lower down, King Con Access is the gateway to a whole face of blue cruising runs, including Eureka, Climax, and Courchevel (Park City's sister city).

The Canyons was once very much the poor relation of the other Park City ski areas. First known as Park West, it had a brief renaissance as Wolf Mountain, when most of the trails were given the names of animals, particularly threatened species such as Cheetah, Lynx, and Ocelot. Purchased

by the American Skiing Company in the mid-1990s, it has been involved in a massive expansion program. Most of the runs were renamed, but the names of some of the lifts, such as Golden Eagle, Condor, and Raptor, survived – no immediate prospect of extinction for them at least.

Another "bird" that over the years has faced financial extinction is Snowbird; although neighbors, Snowbird and Alta have almost nothing in common except liberal amounts of what is marketed as "the greatest snow on earth." It is not uncommon for great storms to close Little Cottonwood Canyon, one of the reasons why it was deemed unwise to involve Snowbird in the 2002 Olympics, and sometimes the resort has to use howitzer shells left over from the Korean war to blast the more avalanche-prone slopes.

While the "Grande Dame" resort of Alta has little in the way of an international reputation, Snowbird, with its huge Cliff Lodge and Inn, looks surprisingly like a purpose-built French ski area and is a destination resort. The key to "The Bird" is its Tram, which speeds 125 skiers and boarders to Hidden Peak at 3300m (11,000ft). From here, the skiing in all directions is high-octane stuff, but fortunately there is one fairly easy way down: Chip's Run, which returns all the way to the base, is a fairly accommodating blue. Everything else, from the black diamond Primrose Path to double black diamonds like High Baldy and Great Scott, is skiing and snowboarding of the gung-ho variety.

Snowbird's magnificent Cirque Traverse is accessed either by the Tram or by traversing from the Little Cloud lift. From the Cirque, twisting and turning past the occasional cluster of blizzard-stunted pine, strong off-piste skiers and boarders can drop off almost at will on either side into chutes like Regulator Johnson, Gad Chutes, Barry Barry Steep, and Mach Schnell. The big new feature at "The Bird" is Mineral Basin, an extensive bowl behind Hidden Peak, which increased the resort's skiable terrain by almost a quarter. A second lift now completes a two-way link with Alta's Albion Basin.

You can also ski Park City, Snowbird, and Alta – and the neighboring resorts of Brighton and Solitude – by sampling the Interconnect, an all-day backcountry tour once known only to "mountain men, wildlife, and a small corps of tight-lipped powder hounds."

FAR LEFT Champions in the making – in the manner of many resorts in the Alps, Park City has a "Kinderschule" where young children can learn the ropes.

CENTER Lights on a bare mountain during the 2001 torchlight descent at Snowbird. This is the way to do it if you don't want to singe your gloves on conventional flaming torches.

RIGHT Not on the torchlight procession route: the joy of leaping off Snowbird's legendary cirques, ridges, and chutes. In deep Utah powder, it almost doesn't matter where you land.

Taos Ski Valley

NEW MEXICO

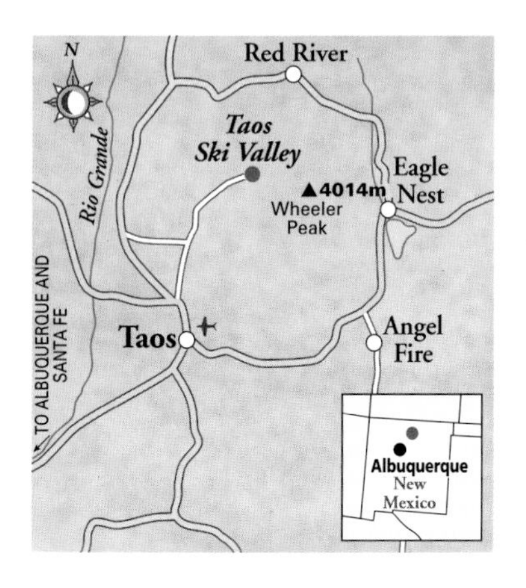

YOU COULD MAKE A MOVIE ABOUT THE STORY OF Taos Ski Valley – Ernie Blake, former German intelligence officer, seeks beautiful location for new ski area. Finds it in – of all places – the Sangre de Cristo mountains, New Mexico, high above the desert home of the Pueblo Indians. Among the first runs Blake cuts are those dedicated to four German army officers who attempted to kill Hitler. Another one honors Sir Winston Churchill. But – skiing in New Mexico?

Snow sometimes even falls in the desert itself, so to find it in abundance in the mountains high above the old town of Taos should not really come as a surprise. The mountains trap clouds over the Sea of Cortéz, which then dry out as they pass over the desert. Taos has a habit of "stealing" some of Colorado's snow and sometimes even its thunder. It is almost as if, like a flock of birds blown off course, snow clouds destined for southern Colorado end up in the Taos Ski Valley.

The snow falls on spectacular terrain, and one of the area's chief attractions is its "steep-and-deep" skiing. Taos also has adequate easy slopes, however, such as Honeysuckle, Bonanza, and White Feather. In fact, close to the daunting-looking Al's Run, which greets new arrivals, there is a sign aimed at reassuring novice skiers that says, "Don't panic. From this point you can see only 1/30 of Taos Ski Valley."

But let's mention the War. It was on July 20, 1944 that the most dramatic circumstances nearly altered the course of World War II – a bomb ripped through the East Prussian headquarters of Adolf Hitler, the so-called Wolf's Lair, during a briefing with senior officers about the deteriorating situation on the Russian front. Although the blast sent debris and smoke billowing into the night sky,

TOP Joaquin Klein lives life to the fullest in the Sangre de Cristo mountains high above the desert in New Mexico.

RIGHT Skiers pause beneath Taos Ski Valley's showcase mountain, Kachina Peak. Ernie Blake, the German-born Swiss who founded the resort, swore there would never be a lift to the summit – skiers face a 45-minute trek along Highline Ridge to reach it.

SMITH

LEFT Taos Ski Valley may not be the biggest resort in the United States, but it certainly has some of the most challenging terrain. The only way to ski it is, to attack!

RESORT	TAOS SKI VALLEY
GETTING THERE:	Santa Fe: 110km (70 miles). Nearest major airport is in Albuquerque: 220km (135 miles), frequent daily shuttle service to and from airport. Taos has small municipal airport.
HEIGHT:	2800–3600m (9190–11,810ft)
NO. OF LIFTS:	12
TYPES OF PISTES:	20% beg, 24% inter, 56% adv.
MAIN ADVANTAGES:	Varied and challenging terrain; good snow record; excellent ski school; new lifts installed recently.
DRAWBACKS:	Limited hotel accommodations; small village; no snowboarding.

demolished the wooden barracks, and killed three officers, the German leader walked away unscathed. In a subsequent radio broadcast, Hitler announced, "A very small clique of ambitious, unscrupulous, and at the same time criminally stupid officers laid a plot to remove me." His would-be assassin, Claus Schenk von Stauffenberg, was later executed.

Ernie Blake, who had sided with the Allies, remained somewhat obsessed with the War following his move to the United States. To him, von Stauffenberg was a hero. He gave his name to one of a clutch of steep gullies that tumbles down from West Basin Ridge. Two more similar steep pitches right next to Stauffenberg were named after other German officers who had opposed Hitler – Oster, for Brigadier General Hans Oster, a key member of the July 20 plot who was also executed, and Fabian, for Fabian von Schlabrendorff, a lawyer and first lieutenant in the reserves who acted as "go-between" among some of the plotters, including Oster. Von Schlabrendorff, the only one of the four men enshrined at Taos to survive, served as Brigadier General Henning von Tresckow's adjutant.

There is one more, much more famous wartime figure commemorated by Blake at his beloved Taos, a British one for a change. Winston Churchill's run is a pretty steep black run, but again, you can reach it by lift.

The resort's most celebrated descent involves a 45-minute trek to the summit of Kachina Peak (3804m; 12,481ft). From here there is a glorious run down Main Street, which finally links with a simple green called Easy Trip. Having paused here for breath, hard-core skiers can continue their downward plunge by taking Hunziker Bowl, High Noon, and El Funko all the way down to the bottom of the Kachina Lift near the Phoenix Restaurant.

Visitors will want to spend a little time in Taos itself, a 30km (20-mile) drive down the mountain. Native Americans have inhabited the site for almost 1000 years, and still occupy a large village nearby. Another Taos claim to fame is its link with D.H. Lawrence and his literary companions and artist friends. The British author lived on a nearby ranch in the early 1920s and his ashes remain there. Taos is still very much a center for arts and crafts, with numerous galleries.

As for Ernie Blake, he died in 1989. Until his death, he ran the ski area like a despot, albeit a fairly enlightened one. He refused to allow snowboarders on his mountain, a policy still in force today. Blake's ashes were scattered from a National Guard jet onto two of his favorite runs, Al's and Snake Dance. And now they are all out there on the slopes, in spirit at least – the officers who tried to rid the world of Hitler, and the man who enshrined their names on his mountain.

TELLURIDE

COLORADO

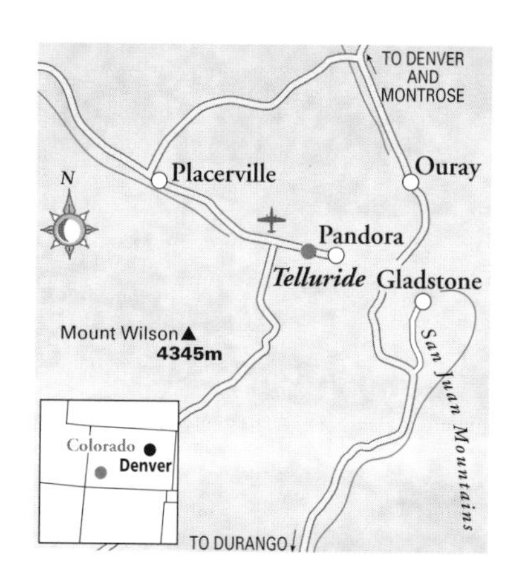

OF ALL THE COLORADO SKI TOWNS, TELLURIDE, at the foot of what the Ute Indians called "the shining mountains," is arguably the most exotic. Spread-eagled at the very end of a spectacular box canyon, it enjoys scenery that is little short of staggering and a history so wild, dangerous, and romantic that Hollywood would scarcely credit it. The historic Wild West town offers some of the best skiing in the Rockies. The Utes who roamed the valley deemed it sacred. Today, many skiers do, too.

Everyone, of course, has heard of Colorado, but strangely the state's most magnificent mountains, the awe-inpiring San Juans, are not a household name. Almost a century ago, they certainly impressed a young bride. Harriet Fish Backus arrived in Telluride in 1906 with her husband, George, who had been hired as an assayer by the Japan Flora silver mine at Tomboy, a mining community high above the town. In her book *Tomboy Bride* she noted, "So high were the walls on the three sides of the valley and so narrow the floor between them that in winter the sunlight reached the little town only a few hours of the day. High above soared the majestic spires of Mount Telluride and Mount Ajax."

But it was not all pure as the driven snow. Harriet also recorded, "Near the main street huddled the houses of prostitutes. All-night carousing in the saloons and gambling dens was evident from the raucous shouting and cursing." Telluride was only shortly past its wildest days. It was the Swedish miners' skill on skis, making a fast descent from the mines at Tomboy down to

TOP A skier gets vertical at Telluride. Some of the runs – such as Mine Shaft, Plunge, and Jaws – are so steep that you can literally see the town between your skis.

RIGHT Ticket to ride: skiers head for the upper slopes of the San Juan mountains at Telluride, one of Colorado's most picturesque ski resorts – "The Most Beautiful Place You'll Ever Ski."

Telluride, that enabled them to be first in line for the services of the "soiled doves." The story goes that there was only one bath in town, owned by a character called L.L. Nunn, credited with supplying Telluride with the first alternating current in the world. Since it was understood that before liaising with local prostitutes a miner would need a bath and a suit, the Swedes were first in line for Nunn's tub, too.

RESORT	TELLURIDE
GETTING THERE:	Denver 530km (330 miles); Montrose: 100km (60 miles); Telluride airport: 10km (6 miles). Bus, taxi, and limousine services from Telluride and Montrose airports. Grand Junction train station: 200km (120 miles).
HEIGHT:	2650–3730m (8690–12,240ft)
NO. OF LIFTS:	16
TYPES OF PISTES:	22% beg, 38% inter, 40% adv.
MAIN ADVANTAGES:	Town close to ski slope; lively downtown area; dramatic setting.
DRAWBACKS:	Difficult access as resort is isolated; limited number of mountain restaurants.

Telluride was also where Butch Cassidy and his "Wild Bunch" carried out their first "unauthorized bank withdrawal," robbing the San Miguel Valley Bank of $24,000 set aside for miners' wages in the summer of 1889. By 1930, with the gold rush over, the Bank of Telluride was on the verge of closure when its president, Charles Waggoner, was jailed after ensuring that his customers did not lose their hard-earned savings. "I would rather see the New York banks lose money," he told the court, "than the people of Telluride, most of whom have worked all their lives for the savings deposited in my bank." By the late 1960s, Telluride was effectively a ghost town.

Thanks to the arrival of the ski resort, times have changed. Indeed, the old Wild West town's respectable present belies its wild and bawdy past. The Silver Bell brothel is now the Ah Haa Arts Center, and the old jail is now part of the Community Center. Telluride has become ever so slightly genteel – except on the slopes, where the spirit of the rip-roaring mining days lives on. Crime is almost unheard of. These days outlaws don't rob banks – they ski out of bounds instead.

ABOVE The two Tellurides – although linked by gondola, neither can see the other, and locals who resisted the modern mountain village agree with the old adage – out of sight, out of mind.

High on the slopes, entirely separate from the old town, a new mountain village has been taking shape for the last decade or so, designed to complement the resort's overall ambience. But old and new do not necessarily sit comfortably side by side, and not everyone in the old town was pleased to see this development.

Two hours away, the resort of Crested Butte, another old gem from the mining days, likes to claim it is "how Aspen used to be and Vail never will be." Telluride's slogan is more definitive: "The Most Beautiful Place You'll Ever Ski."

The skiing at Telluride is exquisite, often steeper than average, but not particularly extensive. There are magnificent steep bump runs, such as Mammoth, Spiral Stairs, and Kant-Mak-M, Franz Klammer's favorite run, which takes its name from the initials of one of the original owners, Ron Allred and his family.

At the other end of the scale, Lifts 1 and 10, the Chondola (a chair and gondola hybrid) and the Sunshine Express serve almost exclusively "bunny" slopes for novices, including Meadows, Double Cabin, and San Joaquin. Another green run, Galloping Goose, is named after an even more extraordinary hybrid than the Chondola. Half railroad engine and half van, this bizarre contraption was still running until the local branch line of the Rio Grande railway finally closed in 1951. There is an abundance of intermediate skiing, including one long, scenic trail called See Forever, from which you can in fact see the distant La Sal range of Utah.

For the last decade, all eyes have been on the exciting backcountry slopes known as Gold Hill and the neighboring Prospect Bowl area. Telluride has finally opened the new area, virtually doubling the resort's lift-served slopes with the addition of three new high-speed quad lifts. One of these lifts now accesses Gold Hill, ending its days as a hike-only destination. Another lift runs to Prospect Ridge and the third takes skiers and boarders into Prospect Bowl itself, where a large wooded area of 328 hectares (733 acres) is already popular with intermediates.

Good restaurants abound and a visit to the "New" Sheridan Hotel is recommended, although you may find yourself sharing the historic old bar with an almost equally historic cowboy on horseback. Now and again a local wrangler called Roudy Roudebush likes to take his horse in there for a quick beer. Telluride is full of surprises – both on and off the slopes.

ABOVE Main Street Telluride at the foot of what the Ute Indians called "the shining mountains." Ajax rears up to 3350m (10,990ft) at the end of the spectacular box canyon.

SALOMON
SKI service
EURO SHOP

VALLE NEVADO, LA PARVA & EL COLORADO

SANTIAGO, CHILE

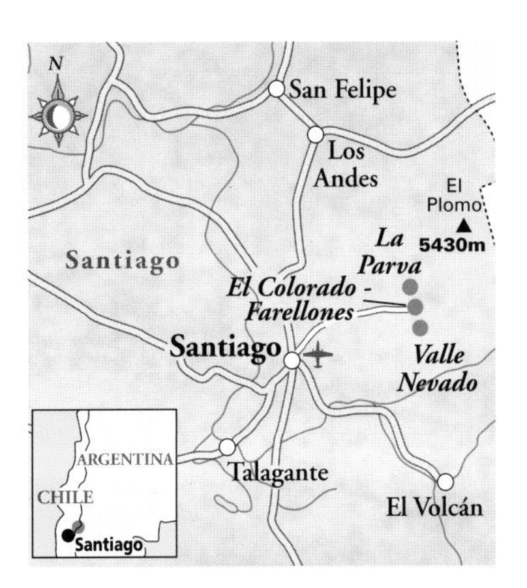

THREE THOUSAND SIX HUNDRED METERS (12,000FT) up in the Andes, a golden triangle of ski resorts shimmers beneath the Chilean sun. The nation's first ski lifts were built here in the 1930s, but this was by no means the first activity in the area. Ancient civilizations once roamed these mountains, and the Incas preserved the mummified remains of their nobility here. Not so long ago, the body of an Inca child was found on the lower slopes of El Plomo, which soars to 5430m (17,810ft).

Today this awe-inspiring peak towers above the twin valleys in which three of South America's best ski areas nestle shoulder to shoulder: La Parva, Valle Nevado, and El Colorado/Farellones. With over 100km (60 miles) of prepared trails and more than 40 lifts between them, together they form the biggest playground for skiers and snowboarders in South America.

This triumvirate is unique in the Andes in offering a European-style playground of linked resorts likened to France's famous Trois Vallées. No other capital city in the world has as much skiing on its doorstep as Santiago, located less than 65km (40 miles) away. The close proximity to the capital, with its Los Angeles-style pollution, produces dramatic blood-red sunsets almost every night on the slopes.

The three resorts are very different in style and terrain. La Parva, named after the "Haystack" peak that overlooks the slopes, is an upmarket resort that provides some of the wealthier Chileans with second and even third homes. It has some of the more challenging and varied terrain, with some good

TOP Skiers enjoy a fondue dinner at La Marmita de Pericles, La Parva, the upmarket Chilean ski resort that provides wealthy Santiaguinos with a convenient getaway from fast-paced city life during winter.

LEFT At first glance you could be looking at a purpose-built resort in the French Alps. It's the main hotel complex at Valle Nevado, at the French-designed heart of Chile's version of the Trois Vallées.

RESORT	VALLE NEVADO, LA PARVA, & EL COLORADO
GETTING THERE:	Santiago to Valle Nevado: 60km (35 miles); Santiago to El Colorado and La Parva: 40km (25 miles). Bus and shuttle services available from Santiago. Book with ski tour agencies.
HEIGHT:	Valle Nevado: 2880–3670m (9450–12,040ft) La Parva: 2670–3630m (8760–11,910ft) El Colorado: 2430–3330m (7970–10,930ft)
NO. OF LIFTS:	Valle Nevado: 9; La Parva: 14; El Colorado: 19
TYPES OF PISTES:	Valle Nevado: 25% beg, 40% inter, 35% adv. La Parva: 20% beg, 55% inter, 25% adv. El Colorado: 40% beg, 45% inter 15% adv.
MAIN ADVANTAGES:	South America's largest ski complex; good snow-making facilities; 1200m (4000ft) vertical drop.
DRAWBACKS:	Very busy on weekends.

off-piste into the Las Vegas gully. Barros Negros is an exhilarating, long intermediate trail. Genuine experts prepared for a short hike should investigate La Chiminea, an almost perfectly formed landmark chute high above the resort, and a steep south-facing wall nearby called La Cara.

Skiing at what is now known as El Colorado was first organized lower down the slopes at Farellones by the Ski Club Chile. Members drove along the old La Disputada mine road to Corral Quemado. Here they would load the mule train for a four-hour ride up to Farellones, where the main run was called La Gran Bajada. According to Chris Lizza, in his *South America Ski Guide*, "Until 1935, when the first refugio was finished, club members stayed in tents erected on the exposed and snow-covered terrain."

Today, Farellones/El Colorado, the biggest individual ski area in Chile, caters mainly to weekend trippers from the capital. The skiing, although

ABOVE Lunchthime at the Jazz Grill where skiers line up for fast food. Those favoring a more sophisticated lunch make for the alfresco restaurant outside the Hotel Valle Nevado.

sometimes fast and furious, is somewhat lacking in variety. There is, however, some dramatic off-piste down rather steep gullies between cliff terrain and the road that meanders up to the French-designed complex of neighboring Valle Nevado. A guide is essential. The steep powder fields of Santa Teresita stretch more than 3km (2 miles), and you will need transport to take you. Other challenging areas can be found low on the mountain in the Corredores chutes, particularly Falso Embudo. The chutes to the skier's right of Cono Este are skiable too, but again a guide is essential – if you end up too far to the right, the chutes peter out into unskiable cliffs.

Valle Nevado, or Snowy Valley – so called because its high, south-facing slopes keep their snow well into spring – is the only true destination resort of the three. Here Americans, Europeans, and Brazilians enjoy luxurious accommodations and extensive slopes in a much more cosmopolitan atmosphere. In 1999 the resort installed the largest snow-making system in South America – almost 6km (4 miles) of pipes serving five lift areas. A year later, Valle Nevado began to implement its master plan, building a 27-unit, 135-bed condominium complex, which broke away from the French-style, purpose-built architecture in favor of a Rocky Mountain flavor.

Chile's first high-speed quad, the Andes Express, has linked the Bajo Cero restaurant with the peak of Cerro Negro (the top of the Peña de Aguila), and a new surface lift has been installed in the Valle del Inca close to neighboring La Parva. These two lifts and new runs have increased the resort's ski area by 25 percent.

With three first-class hotels, six good restaurants (including a superlative alfresco area outside the main Hotel Valle Nevado), and eight modern ski lifts, Valle Nevado relies on attracting an international clientele and actively encourages the idea of skiing around all three resorts. Historically, relations between the other two have not always been so smooth. La Parva and El Colorado tend to regard one another as rivals and El Colorado has in the past tended to treat the three-way link with some suspicion. In recent years, however, this slight tension seems to have eased and you should be able to ski the entire circuit. Skiing from La Parva to Valle Nevado and back is never a problem, but some years you might have to buy a supplementary ticket to make the link to El Colorado and back.

Upmarket and expensive, the Valle Nevado complex overlooks good open-bowl skiing and boarding terrain not dissimilar to the French area of Arc 2000. Although the Valle de Cepo, a vast snowy ravine, is not part of the ski area, there is exhilarating heliskiing here, as well as in the adjoining Valle Olivares.

Skiers and boarders occasionally stray into the Valle de Cepo by mistake and the resort maintains a refuge stocked with basic rations to provide shelter until a search party can reach them. This arrangement came in handy when a senior Argentine diplomat wandered off into the ravine by mistake and was reported missing, threatening to cause a diplomatic incident. Happily he stumbled across the refuge and survived unscathed to enjoy some more skiing on this impressive circuit.

RIGHT El Colorado, where local skiers and snowboarders from the Chilean capital, Santiago, come out to play. It is linked with Valle Nevado and La Parva to form Chile's own Trois Vallées.

PORTILLO

SANTIAGO, CHILE

PORTILLO, SOUTH AMERICA'S OLDEST SKI AREA, IS perched at 2850m (9350ft) just above a collection of blue huts housing Chilean border troops in a remote, steep-sided and quite stunning valley. After a two-and-a-half-hour drive from the Chilean capital of Santiago, visitors must negotiate the desolate Uspallata Pass across the Andes, which links the central valley of Chile with the Argentinean city of Mendoza. This is the most important and impressive of the two mountain passes that remain open during winter. Trucks moving at a snail's pace negotiate hairpin bends to reach the Argentine border just up the road from Portillo, or "Little Pass." Little is hardly the word. The spectacular road runs along one side of the tumbling torrent of the Aconcagua River, while the old trans-Andean railway track, which the road replaced, runs along the other.

Toward the top of the pass, there are 29 consecutive *curvas* (hairpin bends). The lowest chairlift, returning skiers from the bottom of Los Tuneles, crosses the road three times, soaring above Curva 26. Although the line is still in use lower down the valley, up here the rusting track and power lines have long been abandoned. As you follow the Bajada del Tren run you can make a detour and, if sufficient snow has blown in, ski right through the old railroad tunnel that once linked up with the resort.

Portillo is dominated by a single large, yellow hotel and a breathtakingly beautiful frozen lake, the Laguna del Inca. With only 450 hotel beds, the slopes are rarely crowded and you are bound to run into just about everyone you meet more than once – ski racers, tourists, rock stars, and politicians all rub shoulders every night.

TOP Heading for the Laguna del Inca – and hoping for a dry landing! According to legend, the lake was the sacred burial spot of an Inca princess killed on a hunting trip.

RIGHT The yellow hulk of the Hotel Portillo reflected in the tranquil waters of the Laguna del Inca. The lake usually freezes over for most of the season, and skiers who come this far must sometimes cautiously skate back to the ski area.

Uniquely, Portillo has two bizarre but exciting *va et vient* lifts specially designed for accessing the steep chutes in avalanche-prone areas on both sides of the valley, including the celebrated Kilometro Lanzado run where speed skiing was pioneered in 1963.

The larger of the two lifts, Roca Jack, hauls five skiers at a time on linked platters at considerable speed to the top of the chute before suddenly coming to a halt; skiers must then disengage backwards. *Va et vient* lifts are a combination of a conventional cableway and a towerless cable tow. Should an avalanche hit the lift overnight, the cable drops and is buried until it can be located again. From Roca Jack and Condor, its counterpart across the Laguna del Inca, you can ski down to the frozen lake and skate home. Reassuringly, resort-maintenance staff check the depth of the ice regularly.

The restaurant, overlooking the frozen lake, is from another age. Red-jacketed waiters stride purposefully past panelled walls of Chilean oak attending to the needs of diners reclining in leather chairs. It has been likened to the dining room of a great prewar oceangoing liner.

Legend has it that the Laguna del Inca was named after an Inca princess, Kora-Lle, who was killed falling from a cliff during a royal hunting feast. Believing that no human sarcophagus would be suitable for her burial, the heartbroken Prince Illi Yunqui had her wrapped in white linen and buried in the lake. It is said that as her body slowly sank beneath the surface, the water in the lake turned the same lovely emerald shade as her eyes.

RESORT	PORTILLO
GETTING THERE:	Santiago: 160km (100 miles); Los Andes: 70km (45 miles). Bus and taxi services available from Santiago. In season; helicopter shuttle services from Santiago. Book with ski tour agencies.
HEIGHT:	2510–3350m (8240–10,990ft)
NO. OF LIFTS:	12
TYPES OF PISTES:	20% beg, 50% inter, 30% adv.
MAIN ADVANTAGES:	High-altitude lake; beautiful scenery; extensive snow-making facilities.
DRAWBACKS:	Lack of choice for accommodations.

OPPOSITE Hosting the first World Ski Championships south of the equator in 1966 put Portillo on the map. After one race Franz Klammer famously took a dip in the hotel pool, still wearing his skis.
ABOVE High above the last few bends of the mighty Uspallata Pass, Steve Classen gets air on his snowboard in Portillo's remote, steep-sided, hauntingly beautiful valley.

LAS LEÑAS

MENDOZA, ARGENTINA

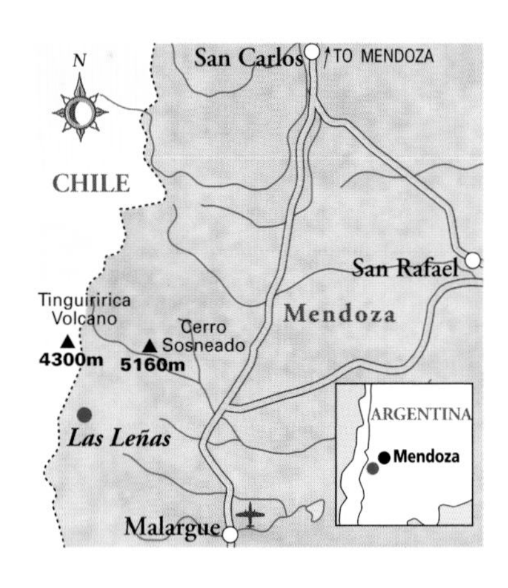

IF ANY RESORT IN THE SOUTHERN HEMISPHERE can claim to mirror the exhilarating challenges of France's Chamonix or La Grave, it is this remote and intriguing ski area three hours south of Mendoza, in Argentina. It all hinges, however, on one absolutely crucial lift: Marte (Mars). This long, steep, windswept chair reaches a high plateau at 3400m (11,100ft) from which chutes of many shapes and sizes fall away in all directions. El Collar and Juno Bowl are major attractions. Sin Nombre and Eduardo's Couloir are spoken of in hushed tones. Some chutes bring you back to the base area; others take you miles into the wilderness to such places as Laguna Escondida. One snowboarder, who enjoyed the Snowboard Park, reported that the out-of-bounds terrain was "outstanding" with snow "so deep and powdery, crashes were a pleasure!"

The Marte chair lift feeds what amounts to a separate ski area, with 40 challenging chutes. If the Marte lift is shut, either because of high winds or avalanche danger, the ski area is reduced to a fairly unremarkable mountain. The remaining 10 lifts serve terrain that has nothing much to distinguish it from any other average mainstream resort, although with skiing as high as 3430m (11,250ft) the area does have a very healthy vertical drop of 1230m (4040ft). As in any rugged resort with steep slopes, extreme avalanche danger often keeps much of the mountain closed.

The remote Las Leñas Valley is at the southern end of the Alta Cordillera opposite the Chilean City of Curicó. The ski area itself lies just south of the spot where a planeload of Uruguayan rugby players accompanied by family and friends crashed between Cerro Sosneado and the Tinguiririca

TOP With so much expert terrain, Las Leñas is regarded as the Chamonix of the Southern Hemisphere. There are good beginner slopes, but these are not what makes this remote Argentinean resort so popular among hard-core skiers and snowboarders.

RIGHT The cliffs and chutes of the backcountry skiing accessed by the crucial Marte lift in Las Leñas are not for the faint-hearted. But for those with sufficient courage and technical skill this remote spot in the Andes provides the ultimate in extreme skiing.

Volcano. Only 16 of the 45 passengers and crew survived, partly thanks to their reluctant decision to resort to cannibalism. Their epic tale was told in the book *Alive* and subsequently adapted into a film.

Ever since it first appeared on the drawing board as a brand-new ski resort, Las Leñas has had an intriguing history. Chris Lizza, a professional ski patroller who spent a month working in Las Leñas, describes some of it in his *South America Ski Guide*. In 1975 the original developers, two brothers who were directors of an Argentinean food and manufacturing company, were kidnapped by Montoneros guerrillas. They demanded a $60 million ransom, which was to be distributed among their poverty-stricken fellow countrymen. After nine months and a partial payment, the brothers were released unharmed. However, they were so affected by their experience that they immediately sold out.

French advisors were called in and in 1983, just a year after the Falklands War between Argentina and Britain, the resort was conceived, somewhat in the image of the more futuristic French ski stations. The principal hotels and lifts (Marte, Apolo, Jupiter, Neptuno, Venus, Urano, and Mercurio) are named after heavenly bodies. Piscis, with a European-style casino and indoor-outdoor pool, is the best hotel in town.

Today the area's finances are somewhat unpredictable. Like so many resorts that are part of the Andean ski industry, Las Leñas has struggled to stay solvent. However, after a record-breaking winter in 2000, the resort set aside an investment of over $1.5 million for a variety of new projects.

For ski purists, Las Leñas is arguably the Holy Grail of the Southern Hemisphere. Lizza's views are unequivocal. "The Marte chair accesses more expert terrain than any other lift on this planet," he says. "Forget the rest of Las Leñas. No skier could ever find – let alone ski – all the possibilities."

RESORT	LAS LEÑAS
GETTING THERE:	San Rafael: 200km (120 miles); Malargue: 70km (45 miles). Domestic flights from Buenos Aires to Malargue; shuttle services available from Malargue airport.
HEIGHT:	2250–3430m (7380–11,250ft)
NO. OF LIFTS:	11
TYPES OF PISTES:	22% beg, 41% inter, 37% adv.
MAIN ADVANTAGES:	Large backcountry ski area; convenient slopeside accommodations.
DRAWBACKS:	Purpose-built resort; lift serving most challenging slopes often closed.

SAN CARLOS DE BARILOCHE

RIO NEGRO, ARGENTINA

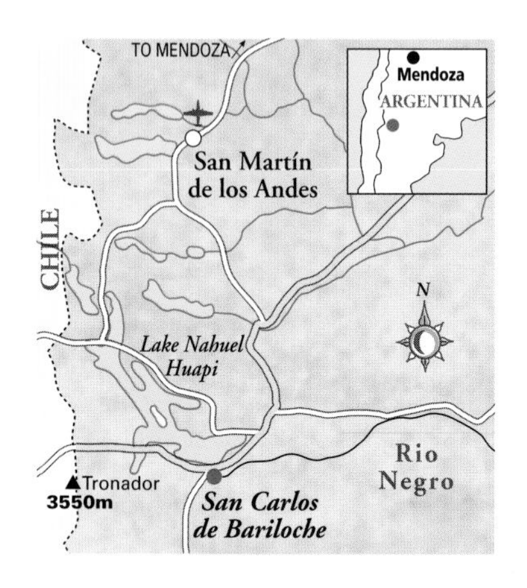

WITH A CERTAIN IRONY, BOTH THE ONSET AND THE termination of World War II had curious repercussions in San Carlos de Bariloche, home to Argentina's biggest, oldest, and most famous ski resort. Somewhere at the bottom of the Atlantic Ocean is a rusting cable car that was destined for Bariloche's dramatic, lakeside slopes. A cargo ship bringing it from Italy was sunk at the beginning of the War and the resort had to wait another 11 years for a replacement. Then, right at the end of the War, a number of fleeing Nazi war criminals sought sanction in this cosmopolitan city. Who knows – perhaps they even skied there.

With a mixed population, which includes people of Irish, Danish, Swiss, Basque, German, Scottish, Austrian, and Italian descent, San Carlos de Bariloche, in the province of Rio Negro, is a truly international city. Founded in 1902 by Germans trading with their fellow countrymen just across the border in Chile, San Carlos received more than its share of European immigrants fleeing from oppression in their own lands – and a few of the oppressors too. With its well-established German population, who had long ago brought Alpine-style chalets and a whiff of *gemütlichkeit* to this part of South America, it was an obvious place to run to during the dying months of the War.

Whether you come by air or road, perhaps crossing the snow-dipped rain forest of the Puyehue Pass from neighboring Chile, you will soon experience a magnificent view of the towering spires of rock that give the ski area its real name of Gran Catedral. You could hardly wish for a more

TOP Although Bariloche's bustling Grand Catedral ski area in Argentina's Lake District can become very busy, it's always possible to find solitude away from it all in the trees.

RIGHT A boarder's-eye view of Lake Nahuel Huapi, near the bustling city of San Carlos de Bariloche. An artist's impression of this spectacular stretch of water was used by Walt Disney to help compile the storyboard for his classic cartoon feature film, *Bambi*.

beautiful setting. Just 20km (12 miles) from the bustling city, perched high above the spectacular lake of Nahuel Huapi ("Island of the Tiger" in the language of the indigenous Araucano Indians), Catedral is all that any Alpine resort in Europe could be: sophisticated, cosmopolitan, and vibrant, with no fewer than eight discos, a casino, and a delightful ski village.

However, things are not always quite as they seem. Until recently, there were various lift companies and ski schools operating their own "territories" on the mountain. With no single overall management, this meant that the standard of the lifts and the grooming varied depending on where you were, and no one took overall responsibility. Today there are just two main lift companies, run by the Robles and Reynal families, as well as two main ski schools. The mountain is effectively divided into two – the Robles side, with its ski school, and the Alta Patagonia side, where the ski school is run by Heini Kempel, a former member of the Argentinian demonstration team.

The name Bariloche is derived from the nearby Vuriloche Pass, used as a trans-Andean corridor by the local Araucano population. In their dialect, Vuriloche means "The people from behind the mountains." Catedral was the first ski resort in the country to install mechanized lifts during the late 1930s. Today, with a vertical drop of 1000m (3300ft), more than 50 runs and over 60km (40 miles) of skiing across extensive, wide-open slopes served by 32 lifts, it is an impressive area.

There has also been a major investment in modern new lifts, including a six-passenger "Superbubble" high-speed chair, and improved snow making. Nearly all of the recent improvements have been carried out on the Alta Patagonia side of the mountain. Here in the Argentinean lake district, the weather can be quite wet and this can sometimes manifest itself as too much rain and too little snow. The snow does come, sooner or later, and in generous amounts, but it can be a long, wet wait, particularly on the lower slopes. Fortunately, Bariloche also has good beginner slopes at the top of the mountain and, in the event of heavy rain at the base, beginners can be taken higher. Only when the rain is accompanied by strong winds do the vital lifts to the higher nursery slopes close, but the main chair at the base area now has 100 percent snow making.

When the rain finally turns to snow in Bariloche, the contrast between the sodden slopes and the colorful vibrant atmosphere when snowflakes pirouette to the Latin rhythms of a line band is dramatic. Après-ski starts there and then with skiers dancing at the base area. The resort no longer has the feel of Britain's bleak Dartmoor in torrential rain; instead the atmosphere is tranformed into something resembling the movie *White Christmas*.

OPPOSITE They're facing the right way for the camera, but the wrong way for the view. Young skiers and snowboarders with Bariloche's beautiful scenic backdrop: Lake Nahuel Huapi.

Towering above the horizon in the distance is the triple-peaked volcanic hulk of Tronador (3550m; 11,650ft). There are three summit areas above the ski slopes. Piedra del Condor – the site of a terrain park with a half-pipe – is located at 1785m (5857ft) at the top of three consecutive chair lifts. The others are Punta Nevada (2090m; 6860ft) and Punta Princesa (2100m; 6900ft).

On the wide plateaus and bowls between these peaks lies a wealth of wide-open, largely intermediate slopes with good, high-speed cruising and abundant off-piste. Lower down, as you enter the more wooded sections of the mountain, there are some excursions in the trees and bushes to be enjoyed by more adventurous skiers.

With Tronador dominating the skyline in one direction and the lake spread out in the other, the scenery is simply outstanding. Unfortunately, this very splendor prompts another curious difficulty facing skiers and snowboarders: the so-called *tira bolas* or snowball throwers. Thousands of students, many of whom have never seen snow before, traditionally flock to Argentinean ski resorts by the busload during school vacations, rent ski suits and moon boots, and ride the lifts to the mountaintop to enjoy the view. They romp in the snow, throwing snowballs at each other, and the idea is to enjoy the mountains and perhaps return the following year to learn to ski or snowboard. The problem is that they can completely dominate the lift system, forming huge lines that vastly outnumber the skiers and snowboarders. The only way the lift operators can properly accommodate "legitimate" mountain users is to ask them to form a separate line and be given priority. The *tira bolas* are big business for the resorts, and skiers and snowboarders might have to concede, albeit grudgingly, that they are a necessary irritation – at least they help finance improvements.

RESORT	SAN CARLOS DE BARILOCHE
GETTING THERE:	Villa Catedral: 15km (9 miles) from San Carlos de Bariloche. Airport and train station in city. Can access from neighboring Chile via scenic Puyehue Pass.
HEIGHT:	1050–2040m (3450–6700ft)
NO OF LIFTS:	32
TYPES OF PISTES:	30% beg, 45% inter, 25% adv.
MAIN ADVANTAGES:	Developed resort with large ski area; good snow-making facilities.
DRAWBACKS:	Unreliable snow record; inconsistent slope maintenance.

Milka
84
Milka
82
DYNASTAR

22

PACIFIC PEAKS

HAPPO-ONE & SHIGA KOGEN, TREBLE CONE, RUAPEHU, JINDABYNE: THREDBO & PERISHER BLUE

And so to the Pacific peaks of Australasia and Japan. Even though the Japanese held the Winter Olympics in 1972 and, much more recently in 1998, few people realize how extensive the Japan Alps are, or that there are literally hundreds of ski areas scattered among these peaks.

Australia seems an equally unlikely location. In fact, many Australians have never even seen snow. Yet this vast continent has several fine ski resorts in the southeastern states of New South Wales and Victoria. They may not be particularly Alpine in nature, but with their ubiquitous forests of eucalyptus, or snow gums, and their colorful birdlife, they provide intriguing skiing.

New Zealand's skiing credentials are well documented. The Southern Alps cover vast distances and are spectacular if significantly lower than the Alps or the Rockies. Apart from some good commercial resorts, New Zealand's "club fields" offer a unique blend of somewhat primitive and low-budget skiing and camaraderie, in stark contrast to the glitzy image skiing has in some parts of the world.

LEFT The ultimate view of the Matukituki Valley, close to South Island's main divide near Wanaka. One of New Zealand's most beautiful and tranquil stretches of water, Wanaka is the gateway to two of the country's biggest ski areas: Treble Cone and Cardrona, as well as prime heliskiing terrain in the Harris Mountains.

HAPPO-ONE & SHIGA KOGEN

NAGANO, JAPAN

IN 1902 JAPANESE TROOPS TRAINING IN THE mountains of northern Honshu suffered a terrible fate. Overwhelmed by a fierce blizzard in the snows of Mount Hakkoda, 199 men from the 5th Aomori Regiments perished. Only 11 survived. Ironically, when war did break out shortly afterward, it ended in a famous victory for Japan – and the country established itself as a major world power.

People are sometimes surprised to hear that Japanese winters can produce a formidable amount of snow. The tragic loss of life that winter's day prompted the Japanese Army to consider providing skis for troops involved in mountain warfare. However, according to documents at the ski museum in Nosawa Onsen, "no one wanted to try skiing, even though Japanese officers living abroad sent skis to Japan upon hearing about this tragedy."

But skiing did finally catch on. In 1911 Lieutenant Commander Lertch began to give lessons at Takada in Niigata prefecture. Japan's first ski club was established in 1912, and by 1923 the All Japan Ski Championships were being held. A pilgrimage to the Japan Alps in 1930 by Hannes Schneider, the pioneer of Austria's celebrated Arlberg technique – to this day the basis of modern skiing – made the sport even more popular.

Today, Shinkansen bullet trains traveling at hair-raising speeds of 270kph (170mph) whisk skiers to resorts all over the country. Depending on which guidebook you read, Japan has between 600 and 700 ski resorts and between 12 and 18 million skiers – this in spite of a recession that has seen the number of visitors slump by as much as 40 percent in some resorts. There are perhaps 25

TOP Bubble with a view – skiers whirr silently to the top of the slopes at Higashitateyama, scene of the 1998 Olympic Giant Slalom and Super-G races. These runs are among the highlights of the "grand tour" of Shiga Kogen's 21 small resorts.

RIGHT A snow-covered Shinto shrine near Shiga; an appropriate metaphor for a nation for whom skiing is almost a religion. Japan has more than 600 resorts and between 12 and 18 million skiers who buy more ski equipment than any other country.

不動尊

LEFT The celebrated "snow monkeys" nonchalantly soak themselves in the warm waters at Jigokudani Yaen-koen (Hell's Valley Park) almost 900m (3000ft) up in the Shiga Heights.

major players, dominated by Shiga Kogen, 40km (25 miles) or so from Nagano, in the Joshin'etsu Kogen National Park. Shiga Kogen cohosted the 1998 Winter Olympics with Happo-one in the Hakuba Valley.

What sets Shiga Kogen apart from its rivals is the extent of its terrain; in reality the resort is a snowy patchwork of no fewer than 21 small ski areas, divided into two major circuits, but all available on the same lift ticket. A short bus trip is necessary to link the two, and the most sensible way of visiting every area is to complete one circuit the first day and move on to the second the following day. A shuttlebus visits every one of the 21 resorts. This means that no matter where and when you end your day on the two circuits, you will be able to get a ride home.

If you add all the component parts of Shiga Kogen together, there are some 670 hectares (1500 acres) of terrain covering about 100km (60 miles) of groomed runs served by around 80 lifts. The area's highest point, the summit of Mount Yoketeyama (2300m; 7560ft), can be obscured by clouds, freezing mist, blizzards, or all three, making it impenetrable. On a sunny day, however, there are wonderful views, and the snow – at a higher altitude than most Japanese ski areas – is usually excellent.

The birch-fronded volcanic terrain in many Japanese ski areas can be intriguingly different from the Alps or the Rockies; there are little cliffs with deep, soft landings, hidden groves of gnarled birch trees, and untracked pockets packed with fresh powder that are rarely skied. Skiing off-piste is still anathema for many Japanese.

Among Shiga Kogen's more interesting runs are the Olympic Giant Slalom and Super-G courses at Higashitateyama. Ichinose is also memorable. There are three Ichinose "resorts" on the circuit, namely Ichinose-Yamanokami, Ichinose-Diamond, and Ichinose-Family.

Nagano prefecture's other main Olympic area, The Hakuba Valley, nestles under the Tsugaike Ridge mountains, which reach almost 3000m (10,000ft) and are as impressive as their counterparts in the Alps. There are half a dozen ski areas dominated by Happo-one, which hosted the Men's Downhill in 1998.

With skiing up to 1800m (6000ft) and a healthy vertical drop of more than 1100m (3500ft), Happo-one has a good mix of terrain and some 35 lifts dotted over the ski area. With a complex system of ridges, plateaus, and valleys you can wander far and wide. Apart from offering some challenging skiing, Happo-one has a strangely attractive base area with a narrow main street winding through Disney-style cottages and chalets with mock-Tudor façades. The broad Princess River flows nearby.

It would perhaps be short-sighted to spend the whole week at "Happo" with so many other resorts close by. The traditional resort of Iwatake has extensive slopes. Hakuba 47 Sports Park offers challenging cruising and good snowboarding terrain. Goryu Toomi has some of the most stirring scenery, including wonderful mountain and river views, and Sunalpina, overlooking Lake Aokiko, should not be missed either.

One evening every winter, each resort in the valley has a fire festival, when the local ski school puts on a floodlit extravaganza on the slopes. Some dress up in traditional costume and descend on ancient hickory skis, others make torchlight descents in formation, and – most dramatic of all – some instructors leap through blazing hoops on skis. The spectacle is accompanied by the hypnotic sound of drums beating at the base of the slopes. Huge crowds gather, many nibbling on a typically Japanese snack: squid-on-a-stick. Perhaps every skier or snowboarder with a sense of adventure should experience the Japan Alps at least once in their lifetime.

RESORT	HAPPO-ONE & SHIGA KOGEN
GETTING THERE:	Matsumoto to Shiga Kogen: 105km (65 miles); to Happo-one: 70km (45 miles). Yudanaka train station to Shiga Kogen: 20km (12 miles); Hakuba train station to Happo-one : 2km (1½ miles). Both have transport services.
HEIGHT:	Happo-one: 760–1830m (2490–6000ft) Shiga Kogen: 1300–2000m (4270–6560ft)
NO. OF LIFTS:	Happo-one: 34; Shiga Kogen: 75+
TYPES OF PISTES:	Happo-one: 30% beg, 50% int, 20% adv. Shiga Kogen: 20% beg, 60% int, 20% adv.
MAIN ADVANTAGES:	Happo-one: beautiful area; good range of ski slopes. Shiga Kogen: hot springs; largest ski area in Japan.
DRAWBACKS:	Happo-one: can be busy on weekends. Shiga Kogen: limited expert level skiing.

TREBLE CONE

CENTRAL OTAGO, SOUTH ISLAND, NEW ZEALAND

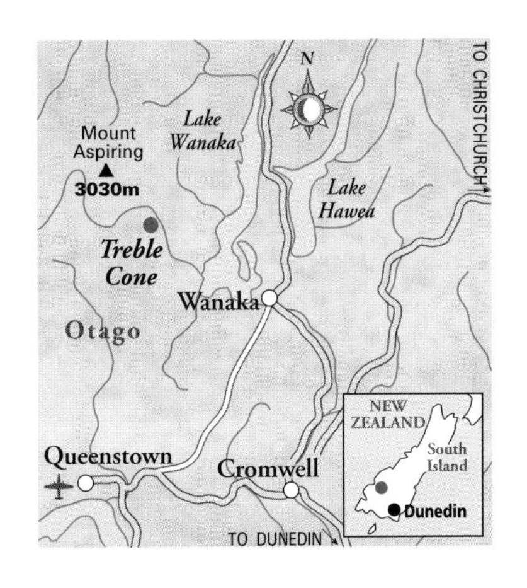

WHEN IT COMES TO THE BEST SLOPES IN NEW Zealand, it's a close call between Treble Cone, arguably the best ski resort in the South Island, and Mount Ruapehu, the mighty volcano that provides just about the only skiing in the North Island. If you throw in the scenery factor, it is probably all even. Treble Cone has stunning vistas across the sublime Lake Wanaka and the Matukituki Valley, complete with a dramatic view of Mount Aspiring (3030m; 9970ft), the highest peak in the region. Whakapapa, the principal resort on Ruapehu, has scenery that is perhaps more awe inspiring but with less of a picture-postcard element. In terms of the weather factor, Treble Cone probably wins hands down – Whakapapa is not known for its blue-sky days. There is also the small matter of the occasional violent eruption from its spectacular crater lake. Suffice it to say they are both inspirational ski and snowboard areas.

One thing Treble Cone has that is absent from the North Island is the bold ground parrot, or Kea. While these comic, green-feathered birds appeal to tourists, most locals view them as something of a pest. They can be seen hopping onto the rooftops of vehicles in parking areas at resorts all over the South Island, using their sturdy crossed bills to tug at anything pliant, including windshield wipers and rubber roof-rack attachments. Stray gloves, picnic lunches, and plastic containers are all tempting and even the electronic wiring on ski lifts is not safe from attack. Keas are protected, however, and moving them or worse, destroying them, can lead to draconian fines.

TOP Here comes trouble – lock everything malleable away if the bold Kea turns up at your ski resort in New Zealand's South Island. This clownish parrot can strip rubber from your windshield wipers, never mind steal your lunch!

RIGHT Treble Cone, the South Island's most challenging ski area, does have lifts! But some skiers are determined to hike to their pet places to get the best "freshies" – and the best scenery.

Apart from enjoying a significant vertical drop of 600m (2000ft), skiers and boarders at Treble Cone can take a 20-minute hike to the very top of the mountain (2100m; 6900ft) where, along with arguably the best view from any ski area in the country, they will find the arrangement of rocks that gives the resort its name.

In addition to long, scenic cruising runs like Outer Limits, ungroomed descents like Sundance, and New Zealand's first six-seater chair, Treble Cone's big attraction is Saddle Basin, with a clutch of enjoyable chutes including Bullet, Shooter, and Super Pipe. Boundary Ridge chutes (not on the trail map) and Powder Bowl chutes complete the menu. There are also two half-pipes, one natural and one man-made. If Treble Cone has a fault in its layout, it is a "cat track," or snow-covered road, which can interrupt the progress of skiers and boarders trying to put together nonstop runs down trails like Gun Barrel and Easy Street.

RESORT	TREBLE CONE
GETTING THERE:	Queenstown: 100km (60 miles). Shuttle bus services available from airport. Wanaka: 20km (12 miles). Daily bus service from Wanaka to Treble Cone.
HEIGHT:	1200–1860m (3940–6100ft)
NO. OF LIFTS:	5
TYPES OF PISTES:	15% beg, 45% inter, 40% adv.
MAIN ADVANTAGES:	Fast six-man chair servicing the area, great off-piste; varied terrain with steeps for advanced skiers; heliskiing possible.
DRAWBACKS:	Access from sea level up dirt track; not ideal for beginners; limited base of resort facilities.

If you really want to rival the Kea and make a meal of your stay, nearby Cardrona is well worth a visit. Although the resort does have some radical skiing – for extreme skiers only – the terrain in general is somewhat more mellow. You could even sign up for a day's heliskiing. Unlike Canada, where the whole heliskiing experience takes place in a snow-covered wilderness, in New Zealand you start from towns like Queenstown, Wanaka, and Methven where snow is quite rare. As often as not, even the helicopter base itself is below the snowline. Returning to green fields and daffodils after the final run can be a welcome change from the desolate expanses of the Canadian wilds.

OPPOSITE Skiers at Treble Cone stop to admire the marvelous views over Lake Wanaka, an oasis of calm compared with bustling Queenstown some 65km (40 miles) away.

ABOVE LEFT Do-it-yourself heli. This run is not on the trail map, but never fear – if you've survived the road to get here, this is plain sailing!

ABOVE RIGHT Intrepid skiers up among the distinctive rock formation at the summit of Treble Cone. They didn't just hike up out of curiosity – there's often great powder skiing from the top.

RUAPEHU

TONGARIRO NATIONAL PARK, NORTH ISLAND, NEW ZEALAND

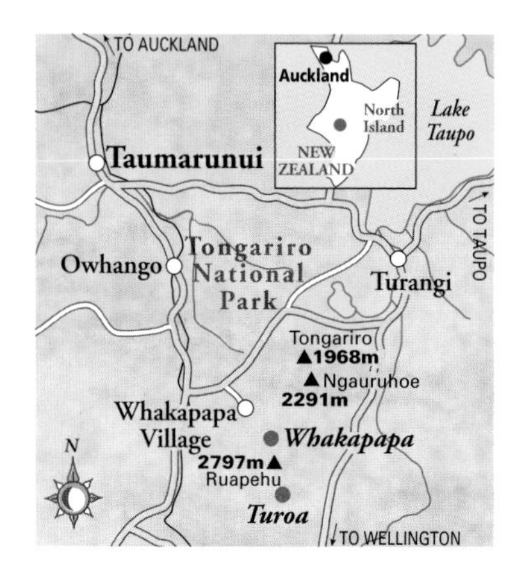

IN 1910 TWO YOUNG RAILROAD ENGINEERS MADE an unsuccessful winter attempt to climb Ruapehu (2797m; 9177ft), a sacred volcano on New Zealand's North Island. They were advised to "procure skis and travel over the snow instead of through it." Duly importing some from Switzerland, they never made it to the top, but were so impressed with the exotic terrain of volcanic gullies, bowls, and walls that they started the Ruapehu Ski Club. It led to the construction of Whakapapa, New Zealand's biggest ski area.

Whakapapa is the Maori term for the "solemn recitation of genealogical ascendancy" – including many spiritual, mythological, and human beings. On a more sinister note, it was also a reference to a tribal battle when the slain victims were laid out for a cannibal feast.

Ruapehu, together with Tongariro and Ngauruhoe, are three awe-inspiring volcanoes standing almost shoulder to shoulder on the central plateau of New Zealand's North Island. They attract bad weather like lightning conductors, and sudden changes in weather and visibility can, in a matter of seconds, turn a blue-sky day into a white-out. The main problem about skiing on a live volcano is, of course, the possibility of an eruption. During one visit to Ruapehu, I recall the mountain manager Scottie Barrie pointing his ski pole up the Turnpike trail toward the crater lake and saying, "If you'd been standing there at 16:57 on September 23, 1995, you'd be dead!" Barrie was not talking about an avalanche, however, but a *lahar*, an Indonesian term for a volcanic slide of water, mud, and ash.

TOP "Kiwis," a.k.a. New Zealanders, may flock to the ski slopes, but the nocturnal flightless bird that gives New Zealanders their nickname is a threatened species rarely, if ever, seen by day.

RIGHT The most stirring sight in New Zealand's North Island is this cluster of awe-inspiring volcanoes – Mount Ruapehu (top left), the perfect cone of Mount Ngauruhoe (center), Tongariro (right), and Taranaki/Egmont (far right).

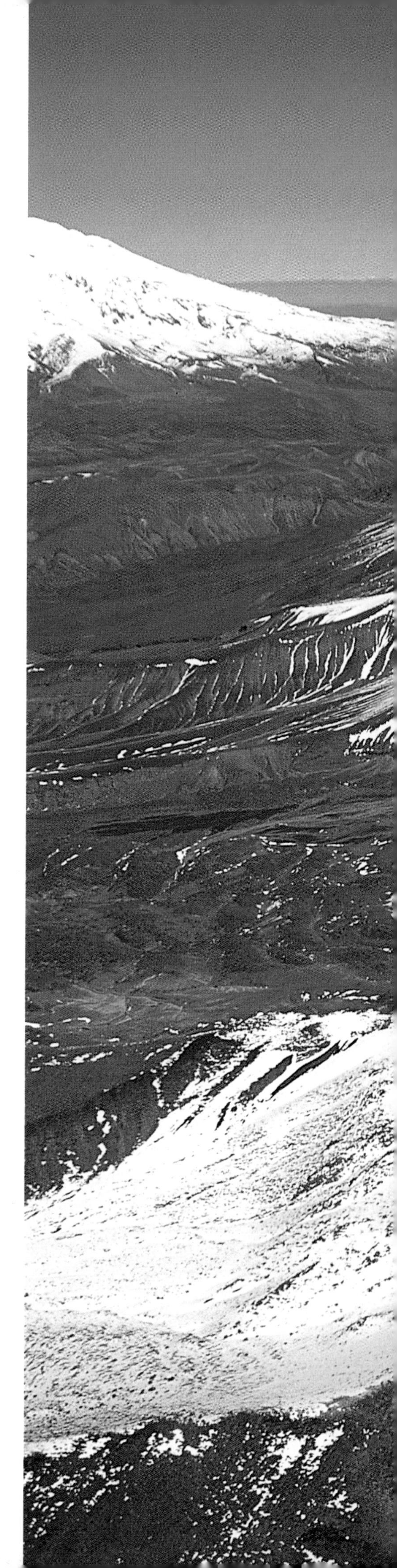

OPEN
50

In normal winters, it is possible to make the three-hour climb to the crater lake and ski down. Fortunately, when the volcano burst into life in 1995, Barrie had already decided to close the lifts. When Ruapehu sent a towering and unstoppable torrent of mud rushing down the mountain, missing the bottom of the Far West T-bar by just a few feet, nobody was in its path. The following year, a series of firework displays spewing vast clouds of dust ruined the snow and delayed opening day, sending the ski area tumbling disastrously into debt. Without mud, the later eruptions, however spectacular and disruptive to skiing, were the equivalent of firing blanks.

In addition to an extensive selection of cruising, Whakapapa has some excellent off-piste in its Black Magic area. But for hard-core skiers, its *pièce de résistance* is the challenging terrain below the magnificent, snow-encrusted Pinnacles. These should be avoided in bad visibility, however, when you can easily become disoriented and fall.

Ruapehu has three ski areas on its slopes – two commercial resorts and a "club field." Whakapapa is the biggest. Its main rival until it went bankrupt a few years ago was Turoa, which opened on the volcano's southern flanks as recently as 1979. In 2001 Whakapapa purchased its neighbor and today the ski area is jointly known as Ruapehu. Although smaller than its more revered cousin, Turoa has some exciting terrain and the biggest vertical drop in Australasia – 720m (2360ft). Avid skiers who want to hike to the top are advised to check with the ski patrol first. From the summit, skiing off Clay's Leap or the Mangawhero Headwall, they will be treated to what one of the country's leading students of skiing, Marty Sharpe, describes as, "475 of the most unforgettable vertical meters (1558ft) in New Zealand."

On the eastern side of the volcano, the third ski area is a small "club field," which has one of the most difficult approach roads in the country – the last 8km (5 miles) to Tukino are only possible with a four-wheel-drive vehicle *and* chains. A glance at Marty Sharpe's *Guide to the Ski Areas of New Zealand* tells you all you need to know about many similar fields. Although Tukino has three on-mountain lodges, the rest makes unsettling reading, "Snowmaking: None. Grooming: None. Ski Hire: None. Lifts: Three rope tows."

RESORT	RUAPEHU
GETTING THERE:	Wellington: 290km (180 miles); Taupo: 100km (60 miles). Auckland: 240km (150 miles). All have airports. Bus and train services available from Auckland. Whakapapa to Whakapapa Village: 6km (4 miles).
HEIGHT:	Whakapapa:1630–2300m (5350–7550ft) Turoa: 1600–2320m (5250–7610ft)
NO. OF LIFTS:	31 combined
TYPES OF PISTES:	Whakapapa: 10% beg, 40% inter, 50% adv. Turoa: 10% beg, 70% inter, 20% adv.
MAIN ADVANTAGES:	Large variety of terrain; interesting volcanic landscape; good boarding facilities.
DRAWBACKS:	Skiing above tree line so can be exposed to wind; no slopeside accommodations at Turoa.

LEFT The Grand Chateau hotel provided a magnificent ringside seat for people observing the pyrotechnic displays when Ruapehu staged a series of dramatic eruptions during 1995 and 1996. RIGHT Whakapapa, New Zealand's biggest and most challenging ski area, isn't all crags and cliffs – it also prides itself on some of the best nursery slopes in the country.

JINDABYNE: THREDBO & PERISHER BLUE

NEW SOUTH WALES, AUSTRALIA

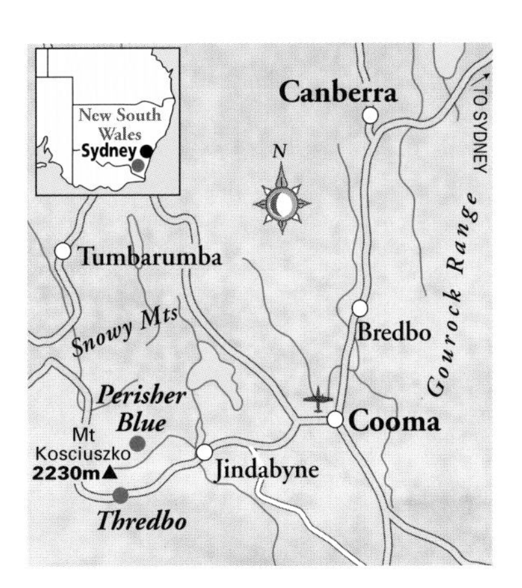

ALICE'S ADVENTURES IN WONDERLAND START WITH a big fall, "I wonder if I shall fall right through the earth," she cries. "Is this New Zealand or Australia?" Had she surfaced in a certain resort near Jindabyne, New South Wales, some of the trail names and ski lifts might have given her a clue: Wombat Walk. Bushranger. Snowgums.

A handful of skiers hurry off to catch a Doppelmayr lift for a final run through the snow gums on the south-facing slopes. From the mountain village, the sound of a zither and yodeling voices drifts across from a bar where locals are warming up for a Tyrolean evening. The warbling of Currawongs is heard as they croon their quirky lullaby, "Quardle Oodle Ardle Wardle Doodle!" Welcome to Thredbo's multicultural melange of cultures, flora, and fauna.

Many Austrians and Czechs came to the Australian Alps to work on the vast Snowy Mountain hydroelectric scheme during the 1950s, and stayed to help pioneer skiing. Two Czechs and an Austrian are credited with starting Thredbo ski village, and have T-bars named after them: Sponars, Karels, and Antons.

Thredbo's mountain is impressive. There are 40 trails altogether and 13 lifts, which include four high-speed quads. On the lower slopes, runs like High Noon Supertrail, Dream Run, and the Crackenback Supertrail cut through the snow gum forest. There is a considerable amount of skiing and boarding in the desolate area dotted with rocks above the tree line. Here T-bars, less likely to be closed by strong winds, rule the slopes. There are several fairly gentle "sightseeing" runs, such

TOP AND LEFT Perisher Blue – the largest resort complex in Australia. In 1995 the neighboring New South Wales resorts of Perisher–Smiggins and Blue Cow–Guthega merged to produce an interlinked ski area served by more than 50 lifts crisscrossing the eucalyptus-lined trails. Blue Cow, Australia's newest ski resort, has the highest slopes and most challenging runs.

as Ego Alley and Albert's Amble, while black runs like Cannonball and Funnelweb provide some serious challenges. With slopes as high as 2000m (6500ft), the resort claims the longest run in the country, almost 7km (4 miles) from Karels T-bar to Friday Flat. Karels is the highest point in Australia to be served by a ski lift, and the starting point for the country's longest downhill race. From here there is a good view of Australia's highest peak, Kosciuszko (2230m; 7310ft), which now lends its name to Thredbo's flagship lift.

It was in Kosciuszko National Park that gold was discovered in 1859. In the depths of winter, prospectors and miners started using planks of wood as primitive skis and in 1861 they held what was possibly the first recorded ski competition in the world. Today it is not uncommon for people to drive for two or even three days to reach the slopes. The miners, bushrangers, cattlemen, and Aborigines who have passed this way can vouch for the thick white blanket that usually covers 11,260 square kilometers (4350 square miles) of snow gum forest. But for those who have never seen snow before, it is something of a leap of faith. I remember well a group of Queenslanders out for their first day on skis, who had encountered not snow but sleet. They were ecstatic. Except for one, who complained of icy slopes. What had she expected? "Well," she replied, "I was hoping it would be a bit fluffier."

ABOVE Way above the tree line on Mount Crackenback at Thredbo – a desolate part of the ski area. The skiing up here is quite easy, however, and offers splendid views across the valley.

According to local folklore, nearby Mount Perisher (2050m; 6740ft) was so named after two cattlemen who found themselves on horseback battling through a blizzard. One of them noted, "The frozen snow was beating into our faces. Jim Spencer's beard was white with snow. Turning to me, he said: 'This is a perisher'!"

The popular Perisher Blue ski resort has a complex history. Built near one of Australia's oldest resorts, Guthega, Perisher, and the linked resort of Smiggins Holes became one of the country's most important ski areas. A mere 15 years ago, a brand-new resort, Blue Cow, opened nearby. Soon Blue Cow had purchased Guthega and the two pitted themselves against Perisher and Smiggins. In the mid-1990s, the media magnate and owner of Perisher, Kerry Packer, bought Blue Cow, combining all four resorts under the Perisher Blue umbrella to form what is probably the largest complex of groomed runs in the Southern Hemisphere.

This presented Thredbo with something of a behemoth of competition almost on its doorstep. Jindabyne, Australia's most prominent alpine town, doesn't take sides, however, providing lodging for skiers and boarders in both camps. Indeed, Jindabyne is perfectly placed for visitors wanting to try the slopes at both Perisher Blue and Thredbo without having to uproot themselves.

Blue Cow Mountain (1990m; 6540ft) shares 13 lifts with its neighbor Guthega, and has some testing terrain and a high proportion of black diamond runs, including Kamikaze and Rock Garden. Guthega has a clutch of exhilarating short, sharp runs such as Parachute, Bloody Mary, and Mother-in-Law.

Although Mount Perisher has the highest chair lift in Australia and prides itself on its Double Trouble double-black diamond trails, some of the terrain is a touch quirky – more like skiing in a valley than on a mountainside. By acquiring Blue Cow and Guthega, however, Perisher added more of the conventional, steep terrain that was somewhat missing.

The only way for incoming visitors to reach the Blue Cow terminal, at the quaintly named Blue Calf mountain, is by train. The Swiss-designed cog-and-rack Ski Tube takes skiers through almost 7km (4 miles) of tunnels on the 15-minute journey to Perisher and Blue Cow from Bullocks Flat. Transport from the Perisher terminal complex to all the lodges is over snow on caterpillar vehicles.

During one of my visits, the lift operator at Murphy's Crossing, which links Smiggins with Perisher Valley, was throwing pink glitter into passing skiers' hair. "Glitter, mate, made by the pixies in the enchanted forests of Jindabyne," he would say, tossing some in the air. "It'll make you turn better, and it's good for the prevention of snow snakes." Only in Australia.

RESORT	JINDABYNE: THREDBO & PERISHER BLUE
GETTING THERE:	Canberra: 180km (110 miles) from Thredbo; Jindabyne: 30km (20 miles) from Thredbo. Snowy Mountains Airport in Cooma: 85km (50 miles); shuttle bus services available from airport; bookings essential.
HEIGHT:	1370–2040m (4490–6700ft)
NO. OF LIFTS:	62
TYPES OF PISTES:	Thredbo: 10% beg, 40% inter, 50% adv. Perisher Blue: 22% beg, 60% inter, 18% adv.
MAIN ADVANTAGES:	Thredbo: Longest vertical drop in Australia; great après-ski. Perisher Blue: Uncrowded pistes; huge ski area.
DRAWBACKS:	Thredbo: Low base depth; lower slopes are often slushy. Perisher Blue: Limited snow making.

RIGHT Mount Crackenback from the opposite side of the valley, wih a glimpse of Thredbo's base area. The lower part of the mountain offers excellent cruising through stands of eucalyptus.

HELISKIING

BLUE RIVER, VALDEZ, MANALI, AORAKI/MOUNT COOK

Helicopter skiing is quite simply the best skiing and snowboarding that money can buy. A lot of money – sometimes as much as $5000 a week, not including international airfares. But forget those James Bond images of daredevils on skis leaping out of helicopters in midair. The helicopter, which does actually land before unloading its wealthy passengers, is simply a taxi service, albeit so expensive that it makes a Tokyo taxi bill seem like a 10-cent bus fare.

You can heliski in many places, from Alaska to Zermatt, but the industry is most highly developed in Canada where the wintry wilderness and lack of environmental restrictions make British Columbia the perfect location. This is perhaps the great joy of heliskiing in the wilderness: the chance to visit places so remote, and in the deep hush of midwinter so secret, that you can chance upon moments of true magic.

RIGHT The extreme edge – a helicopter drops skiers in otherwise inaccessible terrain. Their challenging descent will demand experience, focus, and nerve. And a guide!

Red Bull

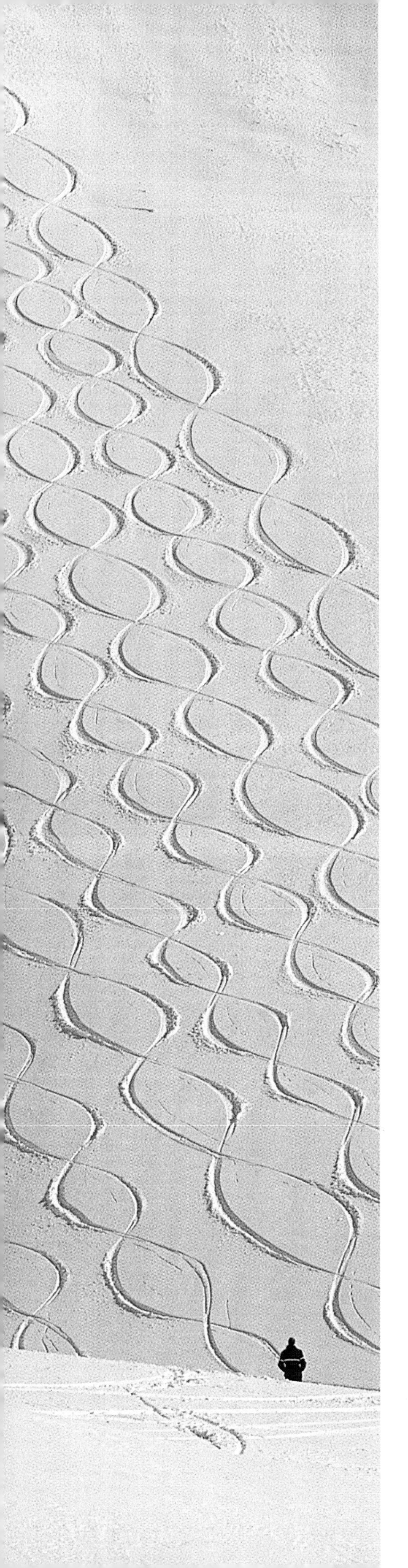

Blue River

BRITISH COLUMBIA, CANADA

Blue River, in a beautiful and remote part of British Columbia two-and-a-half hours from the railroad town of Kamloops, would be a quiet, perhaps dull little railroad stop if it were not for the exciting whomp-whomp-whomp of clattering helicopters. There are no high-speed quad chairs here – not even a solitary T-bar – for this is the home of Mike Wiegele Helicopter Skiing, probably the biggest single heliskiing operation and heliski village in North America – and the world.

Wiegele's territory covers a vast area of 7770 square kilometers (3000 square miles), divided between two mountain ranges, the Monashees (mainly gladed terrain) and the Cariboos (fewer trees), which together encompass over 1000 peaks, many of them with intriguing names. In the Cariboos you will come across Damn Deep, Lion's Paw, Magic Mushroom, Lightning, and Nancy's Relief (famously referring to a notable occasion when a skier named Nancy, in need of a pit stop, finally found a tree to hide behind). In the Monashees' Smoke and Froth Creek zones you can ski Rusty Nail, Yukon Jack, and Blue Angel.

Unlike the typical heliskiing operation from a single wilderness lodge, where up to 44 guests share one helicopter, Wiegele has an entire fleet waiting in a large heated hangar. "The only way to the top around here is by helicopter," says the company. "We are able to offer our guests five Bell 212 twin-engine helicopters, and five of the smaller but still powerful A-Stars." There are usually two main topics of conversation: vertical meters (almost an obsession) and food. Since there is little else to do except ski, eat, and sleep, this is perhaps understandable.

LEFT Enough "powder eights" to make you dizzy. Top skiers assemble each year to compete in Mike Wiegele's World Powder Eight competition; each team of two skiers tries to make perfect figures of eight.

TOP Weather permitting, lunch is taken on the mountain, with "fat" skis arranged to form impromptu seating. You'd be surprised what delicacies the pilot might fly in from the base lodge.

It would be wrong, however, to assume that helicopter skiing is always bliss. When the snow stability is good, the guides tend to select slopes that are steeper. If the rating is fair or poor, they will choose more moderate slopes, and ones that are less exposed to potential avalanches. Fatal accidents are rare, but they do happen. Wiegele's big rival, Canadian Mountain Holidays, with some 10 heliskiing centers in British Columbia, puts it quite bluntly: "We want to make it absolutely clear that there are risks beyond our control that you must share with us."

ABOVE Mike Wiegele's guests are lodged in 23 chalets of spruce and pine logs on the shores of Lake Eleanor, the biggest single heliskiing complex in the world.

RESORT	BLUE RIVER
GETTING THERE:	Calgary: 640km (400 miles); Edmonton: 590km (365 miles); Kamloops: 215km (135 miles); Blue River Airport 1km (½ mile). Courtesy bus from Kamloops.
HEIGHT:	Base lodge: 680m (2230ft) Skiing: 1040–3550m (3410–11,650ft)
NO. OF LIFTS:	Heliski only
TYPES OF PISTES:	All off-piste – intermediate standard up.
MAIN ADVANTAGES:	Stunning scenery; high-quality, reliable, powder snow; tree skiing.
DRAWBACKS:	Isolated location; not suitable for beginners.

VALDEZ

ALASKA

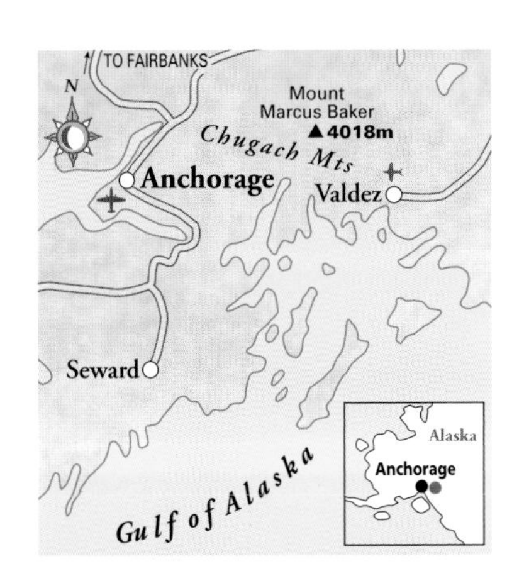

BY CONSENSUS, THE MOST CHALLENGING HELICOPTER skiing is in Alaska. "I tell all skiers that before they die they must experience a week in Valdez. It is like nothing else in the world," says Doug Coombs, founder of Valdez Heliski Guides in the truly awe-inspiring Chugach Mountains.

You would probably never guess that the large and fairly nondescript frontier town of Valdez, perched on the shores of Prince William Sound in the Gulf of Alaska, could generate such excitement – mixed with more than a frisson of fear – among the world's hard-core skiers and snowboarders. The skiing is anything but nondescript; it provides arguably the steepest, most fearsome, and ultimately the most satisfying skiing on the planet. In the early days, safety briefings were carried out in true Alaskan fashion. Legend has it that the pilot carried a revolver, cowboy-style, at his waist. Any client foolish enough to ignore his instructions not to stray near the lethal rotating blades had a warning shot fired at his feet – an effective technique, although it is unlikely that it would find its way into the safety manual of the Canadian Heliski Operators Association.

The more exposed the run, the lower the margin for error, as skiers near free-fall down precipitous couloirs, flanked by columns of unforgiving rock. With its northern latitude, daylight hours in Valdez become sufficient for skiing only from March on, giving way to long days in April and May.

The runs here also have evocative names like Viper or the Berlin Wall. Coombs sold the operation to a fellow guide, Scott Raynor, in 2000, but continues to guide there. He says, "Valdez is

TOP As steep as it gets – at this moment you might be asking yourself: "Do I really want to be here?" Thankfully, even Valdez has a few less dramatic slopes to offer.

RIGHT The Bear – ski it if you dare! Participants in Valdez blaze a trail down slopes of 45 degrees or more where the runs are classified according to their degree of exposure, rather than the conventional system of using colors to indicate difficulty.

H2O
GUIDES
Voilé
SMITH
1-800-578-HELI
Access the Goods

certainly the Mecca for great steep powder skiing. But it is not completely true that the terrain is mostly extreme. Ski films always show the radical slopes skied by the professionals and sometimes we get to guide very good clients down these runs in low avalanche conditions. But we have numerous long, gentle runs, which we ski after big storms, and now skiers are coming for just those kind of runs. About 50 percent of the runs are 35–50 degrees and the rest are 20–40 degrees." Raynor adds, "Forty-five-degree runs in the Chugach with our deep powder can be easier skiing than 35 degrees with no powder."

James Orr, who owns a British company specializing in heliskiing in North America, says, "I still feel the main reason to go to Valdez is to try the steeper runs. Otherwise, why bother going all that way and staying in inferior accommodations? You might as well enjoy the luxury of heliskiing in Canada."

"What makes Valdez unique," Orr adds, "is the fact that even runs that sound less challenging often turn out to be quite daunting. The slopes begin at 45 degrees, an angle occasionally found on short sections of the steepest runs in a ski resort and go up to 55 degrees. For the truly insane, runs of a precipitous 60 degrees can be found, centrifugal force being the only thing keeping the skier in contact with the mountain. And these slopes are not only steep for short sections: the angle is consistently maintained, often over 2000–3000m (6500–10,000ft)," he adds. "Alarmingly for the first-timer, the top centimeter, or sluff as it is known, moves down with the skier creating the unnerving sensation of skiing on a mountain in perpetual motion. Ski Valdez if you dare."

RESORT	VALDEZ
GETTING THERE:	Anchorage: 490km (300 miles). Charter flights to Valdez available, 35 mins by air. Shuttle services to and from Valdez airport offered by all heliski operators.
HEIGHT:	Helicopter drops skiers off at up to 2000m (6560ft) Heli runs average 910m (2990ft)
NO. OF LIFTS:	Heliski only
TYPES OF PISTES:	All off-piste – virgin slopes, tree skiing, glacial bowls, steep mountain faces.
MAIN ADVANTAGES:	Unspoiled locations; snowcats often available if helicopters unable to fly; fabulous snow.
DRAWBACKS:	Not suitable for beginners; remote location.

LEFT In Valdez you might feel happier checking out the slopes from a distance. There's always another day – as the guides are always saying: "The mountains ain't going nowhere. They'll still be here tomorrow."

MANALI

HIMACHAL PRADESH, INDIA

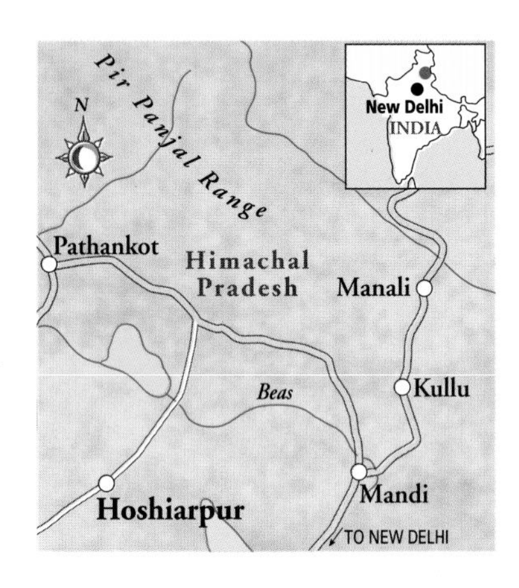

AN EQUALLY DRAMATIC LANDSCAPE AWAITS HELISKIERS in the Indian state of Himachal Pradesh. High in the Pir Panjal range, not so far from the Tibetan border, the glacial River Beas cuts its way through the Valley of the Gods, rushing alongside the narrow streets of Manali, a teeming, cacophonous, and colorful trekking center. The river causes frequent landslides, which pile rocks along the wayside approaches to this bustling small town.

A relatively prosperous place (by Indian standards), Manali is at the head of the fertile Kullu Valley, famous for its apples, plums, cherries, pears, apricots, and red rice. Ancient timbered farmhouses dot the rolling fields and orchards on the outskirts of town. "From certain places in our operating area the view is as grand as that from the summit of Mount Everest," says Roddy Mackenzie, the Australian owner of Himachal Helicopter Skiing (HHS). "However, as our guest, you can save yourself a long walk. No comparison with ranges outside Asia can convey the grandeur of the Himalaya. Peaks as high as 6500m (21,300ft) form a fortress against the winds to ensure that we ski on consistent, light powder snow at the lower elevations." But HHS stresses that, "a day off due to bad weather is never boring." Visitors can trudge through the snow to town, or visit the rustic farmhouses of old Manali. There are any number of genuine monasteries and temples in the vicinity.

Helicopter departures provide a moment of wonder for local children. Bright-eyed with excitement, some carrying homemade skis, they have to be shooed away from the helipad by the ground crew as the powerful Lama or Bell 407 rises slowly from its snowy perch.

TOP Ancient timbered farmhouses, quite unlike what you might expect from India, dot the fields and orchards on the outskirts of town. Unlike heliskiing lodges in Canada, there's plenty to explore if bad weather prevents skiing in Manali.

RIGHT The surreal excitement of skiing at up to 5000m (16,400ft) in the Himalaya with Himachal Helicopter Skiing is hard to beat. Thanks to "fat" skis (wide skis that float on the surface of the snow), almost any fit intermediate skier can enjoy heliskiing.

As the helicopter nears a picturesque high mountain valley or a desolately beautiful snowfield, at altitudes approaching 5000m (16,400ft), an astonishing sight confronts the passengers. Way above and beyond the landing area, gigantic peaks like Deo Tibba, Indrasun, and Mukherbay soar to impossible heights, all over 6000m (19,600ft). On this scale, peaks like the Matterhorn and Mont Blanc would be little more than foothills. The effect is mesmerizing, especially when the helicopter has swooped off to collect the next group of skiers, leaving the first group overwhelmed by silence before they finally tear themselves away to start their descent.

The skiing here can be sublime. With a tree line reaching 3400m (11,100ft), you find yourself floating effortlessly through rhododendron bushes while the sun peeps through vaulted ceilings of Himalayan oak and stands of silver birch. With any luck you will encounter yellow-billed blue magpies and golden eagles soaring above you. On occasion, you may even see a white wolf padding through a nearby snowfield. Many runs have evocative, hybrid names that reflect both the locale and the influence of Western heliskiing – Mondo Thach, Chandertal Cruise Basin, Chhaki Nal, Ali Ratna, Nay Nay Baba, and Enchanted Forest. Others, like Rock 'n Roll, I Don't Know, and Nasty Nick are decidedly less spiritual in tone.

Apart from superb heliskiing, Manali has its own tiny local ski area called Solang Valley, which advises its clients: "Saris and gents suits should be avoided." This probably applies to the heliskiing operation, too.

RESORT	MANALI
GETTING THERE:	New Delhi: 500km (310 miles); Bhuntar: 50km (30 miles). Flights from New Delhi to Kullu; 1hr drive from Kullu to Manali; bus and taxi services available from Bhuntar and Kullu.
HEIGHT:	Skiing as high as 5030m (16,500ft)
NO. OF LIFTS:	Heliski only
TYPES OF PISTES:	All off-piste.
MAIN ADVANTAGES:	Beautiful range of mountains; culturally interesting; light, dry snow.
DRAWBACKS:	Not suitable for beginners; bad weather affects flying times; high fitness level required.

LEFT Local women pose for the camera with a powerful Lama helicopter in Manali. These huge racing skis are purely picture perfect; you wouldn't get very far on them in the deep snow.

AORAKI/ MOUNT COOK

CANTERBURY, SOUTH ISLAND, NEW ZEALAND

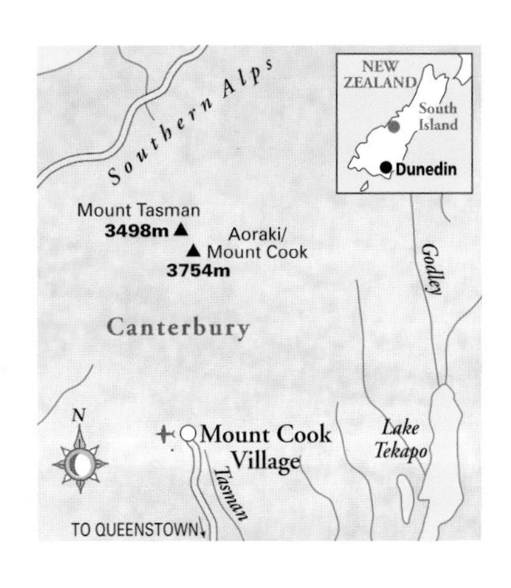

NEW ZEALAND'S SOUTHERN ALPS MAY NOT BE QUITE in the same league as the Himalaya, but they are dramatic nonetheless. The Aoraki/Mount Cook region features some of the country's highest mountains and most dramatic glaciers. When the Polynesians arrived here from the tropical Pacific, they risked frostbite and dangerous mountain rivers to gaze out on the highest mountain in their new homeland, naming it Aoraki. Endearingly, a nearby glacier (now known as the Franz Josef glacier) was called Ka Roimata o Hinehukatere, or the Tears of the Avalanche Girl.

According to Maori legend, Hinehukatere persuaded her lover, Tawe, to go climbing with her but he slipped and fell to his death. Heartbroken, Hinehukatere's tears froze to form the glacier. In spite of a large chunk that fell from its summit a few years ago, Aoraki/Mount Cook (3754m; 12,315ft) – with its attendant snowfields and glaciers – is still the highest and most impressive of New Zealand's myriad peaks. It is a truly awe-inspiring mountain, with weather to match – rarely does one blue-sky day follow another. Sometimes a blue-sky hour is a rarity.

Aoraki/Mount Cook was first climbed on Christmas Day, 1894, and early tourists took guided trips to the glaciers to admire the views, enduring a rough horse-drawn coach ride to reach Huddleston's Hermitage. The first cars arrived in 1906, equipped with telephones in case of emergency. The first recorded car trip lasted 22 hours and when the exhausted travelers finally arrived at the Hermitage Hotel in Mount Cook Village, they found the staff sound asleep. In 1922 the Mount Cook Company was set up to run the tourism program – its slogan: "Thousands of Feet Above Worry Level."

TOP Deep in the wilds of Aoraki/Mount Cook National Park – Hooker Lake, with a backdrop of majestic alpine scenery. Twenty-two of New Zealand's highest peaks are to be found here.

RIGHT Popping out of the ice – a skier with Ski Plane Alpine Guides emerges from one of the safe crevasses on the Tasman Glacier. Skiers arriving by skiplane usually take one or possibly two descents down a fairly easy 12km (7½-mile) run.

Although Aoraki/Mount Cook and Mount Cook Village featured prominently in New Zealand's early skiing history, it has no ski area as such today. Instead, it is accessed by skiers and boarders who arrive on its slopes by helicopter or light planes fitted with skis. Aoraki/Mount Cook National Park, in some ways reminiscent of Chamonix's grandeur, covers an area of nearly 7000 hectares (17,300 acres) of majestic alpine scenery, a third of which is gripped by permanent snow and ice. Twenty-two of New Zealand's 27 peaks in excess of 3000m (10,000ft) are to be found here.

Alpine Guides, based around the Main Divide in the center of the Southern Alps, runs its Wilderness Heliski operation with the Helicopter Line in the Liebig and Malte Brun Ranges and the Tasman and Murchison Valleys. The guides also accompany skiplane flights with Mount Cook Skiplanes from Mount Cook Village to New Zealand's largest glacier, the Tasman, named after the Dutch explorer Abel Tasman. The first "flight-seeing" skiplane, a wooden Auster, landed on the glacier in 1955. Today, Mount Cook Skiplanes operate a fleet of Cessna and Pilatus Porter aircraft all year round.

Some individual heliski runs provide a vertical drop of as much as 1500m (5000ft). But a typical day's heliskiing would involve three or four descents totalling around 3000m (10,000ft). Wherever you are, being air-lifted to remote, awe-inspiring mountain wildernesses is often a spiritual as well as a thrilling experience. Your Mount Cook Skiplane guide will almost certainly let you explore one or two safe cavernous crevasses with domed ceilings of ice. Yet another moment of true magic.

RESORT	AORAKI/MOUNT COOK
GETTING THERE:	Christchurch: 330km (200 miles); Queenstown: 270km (170 miles); Tekapo: 100km (60 miles). Daily flights to Mount Cook from Christchurch and Queenstown. Mount Cook Village has own small airport for limited domestic traffic.
HEIGHT:	Aoraki/Mount Cook: 3754m (12,315ft)
NO. OF LIFTS:	None, just heliskiing
TYPES OF PISTES:	Suitable for intermediate to advanced off-piste skiers.
MAIN ADVANTAGES:	Fantastic off-piste skiing on Tasman Glacier and surrounding terrain; beautiful dramatic scenery.
DRAWBACKS:	Suitable only for off-piste skiing. Poor weather can prevent uplift of helicopters.

LEFT Clutching an ice axe high in the sky, this snowboarder seems in tune with Sir Edmund Hillary, who often climbed in the Aoraki/Mount Cook area before his conquest of Everest.

INDEX

INDEX

Photographic Credits

Copyright rests with the following photographers and/or their agents.

Key to Locations: t = top; tl = top left; tc = top center; tr = top right; b = bottom; bl = bottom left; bc = bottom center; br = bottom right; l = left; r = right; c = center. (No abbreviation is given for pages with a single image, or pages on which all photographs are by same photographer.)

Photographers

A .... Atlas / **FO** = Faith Ozenbas; **ZK** = Zafer Kizilkaya
AA ..... Ace & Ace / **EH** = Esben Hardt
AAP ... Action & Adventure Productions /
.... **SE** = Soren Egeberg)
AC ..... Adam Clark
BBD .. Bildagentur Buenos Dias
BF ...... Baumann Fryberg
BM .... Buddy Mays
BS ...... Brett Schreckengost
BWR .. Brian W. Robb
CD .... Christopher Dolmitter
CI ...... Corbis Images
CL ..... Cameron Lawson
CS ..... C. Sonderegger
DB ..... David Brounell
DE ..... Don Eastman
DW .... David Wall
EN...... Edmund Nägele
GR ..... Glenn Randall
GVD... Greg Von Doersten
HG ..... Henry Georgi
JC ...... Juan Castro
JHSA .. Jackson Hole Stock Agency
JK....... James Kay
KTB.... Kitzbühel Tourist Bureau
LP....... Larry Prosor
MF ..... Mattias Fredriksson
MG .... Mark Gallup
MS ..... Mark Shapiro
TO...... Terry Oakley
PM ..... Paul Morrison
R .... Rapsodia / **LB** = Laurent Bouret
RM..... Robert Millman
S......... Spectrum / **SON** = Seon O'Neil;
.... **HK** = Henry Kalen; **MN** = Mark Newman
SM ..... Scott Markewitz
SS....... StockShot / **JC** = J. Clyde; **GP** = Gary Pearl;
.... **NY** = Nick Yates; **TH** = Tony Hairington
SZ ...... Stefano Zardini
TT ...... Tim Thompson
V........ Venturepix / **MJ** = Mark Junak

Page	Location	Credit
Endpapers	l	S/HK
1		SM
2		R/LB
4		SM
6-7		AC
7		SS
9		CI
10	tl	JK
10	tr	S/SN
10	bl	BWR
10	cr	SM
10	br	CD
11		A/FO
14–16		BWR
17	l	A/FO
17	r	R/LB
18		SS/JL
19		R/LB
20		GVD
21		BWR
22	t	AC
22	b	GVD
23		BWR
24		BM
25–26		V/MJ
27–29		GVD
30		AAP/SE
31–32		BWR
33		AA/EH
35		KTB
36		BBD
37–38		SM
39		A/ZK
40–43		HG
44		SS/JC
45		AC
46		HG
47	l	A/ZK
47	r	AA/EH
48		AA/EH
50–51		HG
52		A/ZK
53		HG
54		CS
55		BF
56		EN
57–58		A/ZK
59	l	BWR
59	r	SM
60		SM
61–65		SZ
66–68		MF
69	l	MF
69	r	GVD
70		GVD
71		MF
72–74		SM
75–76		PM
77	l	S/MN
77	r	HG
78		SS/GP
80		HG
81	l	HG
81	r	GVD
82–83		HG
84		BWR
85		SS/NY
86		RM
87		DB
88		JHSA
89–90		SS
90		LP
91–92		LP
94		TT
95–98		SM
99		AC
100		CL
101		SM
102–104		SM
105	l	BS
105	r	DE
106–107		BS
108		GVD
109–110		GR
111		MG
112–114		GR
115		GVD
116–117		SM
118		JC
119		MG
121		JC
122		DW
124–126		CD
127	l	DW
127	r	MF
128–129		MF
130–133		DW
134–137		TO
139		SS/TH
140–142		LP
143–144		SM
146–148		JK
149	l	SM
149	r	JK
150		LP
152–153		GVD
154		MS
159		AC

ACKNOWLEDGMENTS

Every book is the result of teamwork, and I would like to thank the
550 ski areas and innumerable tour operators,
tourist offices, and airlines which have hosted me during almost
30 years on and off the world's pistes.

In particular I would like to thank my wife, Vivianne,
who in spite of being Swedish, has sometimes corrected my English,
Vanessa Haines of the Ski Club of Great Britain who did much
of the fact panel research, and my *Financial Times* colleagues
Max Wilkinson, Peter Whitehead, and Jill James for indulging my
global wanderings in the mountains over the years,
particularly during my 365 consecutive days on skis in 1994.

Thanks also to Franz Klammer, Minty Clinch, James Orr, and especially my editor, Ingrid Corbett.